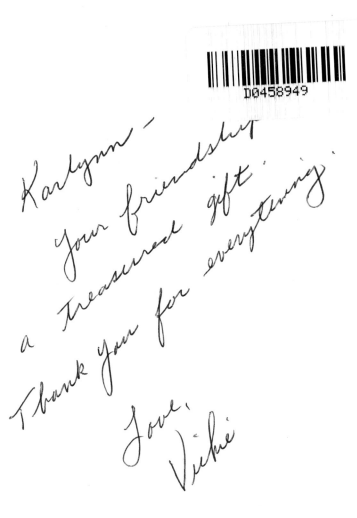

Karlynn —

Your friendship

a treasured gift.

Thank you for everything.

Love,
Vickie

KEEP GOING

OTHER BOOKS BY JOSEPH M. MARSHALL III

Soldiers Falling into Camp: The Battles at the Rosebud and the Little Big Horn (co-author)

Winter of the Holy Iron

On Behalf of the Wolf and the First Peoples

The Dance House: Stories from Redbud

The Lakota Way: Stories and Lessons for Living

The Journey of Crazy Horse: A Lakota History

How Not to Catch Fish: And Other Adventures of Iktomi

Walking with Grandfather: The Wisdom of Lakota Elders

KEEP GOING

The Art of Perserverance

#

Joseph M. Marshall III

Sterling Publishing Co., Inc.
New York

Published by Sterling Publishing Co., Inc.
387 Park Avenue South, New York, NY 10016
© 2006 by Joseph M. Marshall III
Distributed in Canada by Sterling Publishing
c/o Canadian Manda Group, 165 Dufferin Street
Toronto, Ontario, Canada M6K 3H6
Distributed in the United Kingdom by GMC Distribution Services
Castle Place, 166 High Street, Lewes, East Sussex, England BN7 1XU
Distributed in Australia by Capricorn Link (Australia) Pty. Ltd.
P.O. Box 704, Windsor, NSW 2756, Australia

Manufactured in the United States of America

ISBN-13: 978-1-4027-3607-0

Book design by Carol Petro

To the memory of

Dru Sjodin

1981–2003

and

Jancita Eagle Deer

1951–1975

and

To all of the strong-spirited people

who endured Hurricane Katrina

and are teaching the rest of us how to

keep going.

CONTENTS

PROLOGUE: The Question 1

CHAPTER ONE 7

CHAPTER TWO 21

CHAPTER THREE 49

CHAPTER FOUR 67

CHAPTER FIVE 99

CHAPTER SIX 107

CLOSING 119

A young man asked his grandfather why life had to be so difficult sometimes. This was the old man's reply.

Grandfather says this: "In life there is sadness as well as joy, losing as well as winning, falling as well as standing, hunger as well as plenty, badness as well as goodness. I do not say this to make you despair, but to teach you reality. Life is a journey sometimes walked in light, sometimes in shadow."

Grandfather says this: "You did not ask to be born, but you are here. You have weaknesses as well as strengths. You have both because in life there is two of everything. Within you is the will to win, as well as the willingness to lose. Within you is the heart to feel compassion as well as the smallness to be arrogant. Within you is the way to face life as well as the fear to turn away from it."

Grandfather says this: "Life can give you strength. Strength can come from facing the storms of life, from knowing loss, feeling sadness and heartache, from falling into the depths of grief. You must stand up in the storm. You must face the wind and the cold and the darkness. When the storm blows hard you must stand firm, for it is not trying to knock you down, it is really trying to teach you to be strong."

Grandfather says this: "Being strong means taking one more step toward the top of the hill, no matter how weary you may be. It means letting the tears flow through the grief. It means to keep looking for the answer, though the darkness of despair is all around you. Being strong means to cling to hope for one more heartbeat, one more sunrise. Each step, no matter how difficult, is one more step closer to the top of the hill. To keep hope alive for one more heartbeat at a time leads to the light of the next sunrise, and the promise of a new day."

Grandfather says this: "The weakest step toward the top of the hill, toward sunrise, toward hope, is stronger than the fiercest storm."

Grandfather says this: "Keep going."

⊹

PROLOGUE

The Question

A few years ago a young man named Jeremy learned that his father, Jeremy Sr., had cancer. The doctors warned the younger Jeremy and his family that the disease had not been detected in its early stages. Nevertheless, as people often do in the face of obvious hopelessness, the young man and his family prayed for a miracle.

The doctors, for their part, did the best they could. But the surgery and subsequent treatment only seemed to exacerbate an already difficult situation. Jeremy helplessly watched as his father's condition deteriorated swiftly and he wasted away. The miracle his family desperately hoped for didn't come.

On a cool spring night Jeremy's father departed on his journey to the spirit world. And, in the months that followed, the young man was beset by a swirl of grief, confusion, and anger. Questions and issues about life and death overwhelmed him.

As a teacher of history, Jeremy spent his time and energy, for nine months of the year, on students, lesson plans, reading and correcting papers, and an apathetic principal more concerned with policy and dotting i's and crossing t's than in replacing woefully outdated textbooks. Jeremy relished the summers when he could play softball and read books he didn't have the time for during the school year.

As a teacher he was experienced enough to write lesson plans and endure the mountains of paperwork, and was mostly successful in engaging students invariably turned off by history. And he somehow looked forward to crossing intellectual swords with the principal, to face the challenge of the man's obstinacy and narrow-mindedness.

But as a young man he had already learned that life and death were realities for which there were no easy answers. Jeremy knew only one thing for certain: He had not lived long enough to find the right answers.

So he reached out to the one person in his life who always seemed to have an answer.

To his friends he was known as Old Hawk, but to his family he was simply Grandpa. Old Hawk was well past eighty. He had never traveled more than four hundred miles in any direction from where he'd been born. But that mattered little, because, as Old Hawk knew well, life itself was the greatest journey.

Old Hawk knew that the roads traveled in this life imparted lessons that experientially, emotionally, and spiritually were greater than the number of hills climbed, or the borders crossed. They were greater than the turns made, or the horizons waiting ahead. He knew that the most important and enduring lessons come from the difficult roads, those that twist and turn, are narrow and dark, and filled with challenges and obstacles. Roads easily traveled offer no travail and, therefore, no sense of achievement, because anything easily attained offers little value in return.

Old Hawk had no formal education to speak of and though he knew a little English, he preferred the familiarity of his native tongue. His hair was gray and his face weathered from sun and storm. The rich brown hue of his skin was testament to his native heritage. His hands were still strong, though bent and scarred from a lifetime of hard work. In his life Old Hawk had plowed and planted, was a trainer of horses, a hunter, and a builder of houses. He had lost count of the thousands of postholes he had dug to build fences, and likewise the number of posts he had placed in the Earth. He had known disappointment, heartache, sadness, and loss as well as the satisfaction of a job well done and the resolve of clinging to his beliefs and principles in the face of temptation and ridicule. In many, many ways he was like most men, most people. But to Jeremy, Old Hawk was his grandfather and, therefore, like no other.

Two characteristics always drew young Jeremy to his grandfather: a quiet demeanor and a steady gaze in his eyes, no matter what the situation.

Jeremy had spent most of his formative years with his grandparents, and he could not remember a single instance during childhood when his grandfather had raised his voice in anger. No matter the problem, crisis, or circumstance, the old man always faced it with a quiet resolve. Perhaps that was the reason there was always peacefulness in his eyes, like the stillness of a deep, quiet pool of water.

So one day Jeremy went to his grandfather carrying his grief and confusion as if it were all the heartaches of the world.

The old man took him to the shade of an old cotton-wood tree where they sat and listened to the gentle rustling of the soft breeze among the leaves.

"Since I was a boy, the sounds of cottonwood leaves in the wind remind me of my mother's voice," Old Hawk began. "But then I think that somehow it could also be the voice of God."

Jeremy listened for several moments, but for the life of him all he could hear was the leaves rustling.

"So, Grandson," the old man went on, "I can see by the look on your face that you are troubled. There seems to be something pulling down at your heart."

So the young man asked his question. It was the same question that he had asked several times before and in many different ways. But the anguish and confusion from which it came was always the same.

"Grandpa, why is life so difficult?"

ONE

Looking up at the rustling leaves, or perhaps past them, Old Hawk listened to their bright song again, and then turned to his grandson.

"I am an old man," he said. "I've seen something of life, but I don't know if there is one answer that will satisfy you. I think there are many answers out there waiting for you to find them. And I do know this: Life is not easy. But that is the way it is and we cannot change it. The only thing we can do is try to understand it."

Jeremy was not surprised by the answer. He knew his grandfather had a way of providing answers that had to be found, or earned.

"How can you be so certain of these things?" Jeremy asked. "There are times when I think it would be far easier to accept pain and what life brings, rather than try and understand it."

"I know these things because I have traveled a long way down the road we call life." The old man pointed. "You're still at the beginning. And at the beginning, we don't know anything. At the end, we have experience to draw on, and my experiences tell me that there is more to life than simply accepting it."

"But don't you still wonder about life?" Jeremy insisted. "Lately, that's all I've done. So I guess what I'm really asking is: Why do bad things happen? Didn't you ask those kinds of questions when you were young?"

"Yes, I did. I asked my father and my grandfather," answered Old Hawk.

"What did they say?" Jeremy wanted to know. "What did your grandfather say to you when you asked these same questions?"

"He told me to make the journey that lay ahead of me, the journey that would be my life. That was the only way, he said, that I would learn."

Old Hawk paused and Jeremy leaned forward in anticipation, eager and desperate for the conversation to continue. He noticed that the leaves above them seemed to rustle a little louder.

"Grandfather says this," Old Hawk began . . .

"In life there is sadness as well as joy, losing as well as winning, falling as well as standing, hunger as well as plenty, badness as well as goodness. I do not say this to make you despair, but to teach you reality."

Old Hawk rubbed his palms together, as he always did when he had something important to say. It was a gesture Jeremy had known since childhood. Sometimes what had followed was cold, hard truth, and yet somehow there was also reassurance. Furthermore, though the old man did know more English than he would admit to, he always resorted to his native tongue whenever he wanted to leave a lasting impression on his grandson. And whenever he spoke in his native tongue, not only was there clarity, but eloquence as well.

Old Hawk began to speak.

"Life wears two faces and one is no less real than the other.

"If everything were the same all of the time, there would be no variety, no excitement, and no balance. There would be no black to offset white, no sunset to finish the day that began with sunrise, and no warmth to chase away the cold. But that which gives your journey balance throughout this life also brings difficulty. In the end, it also brings a gift we often do not see.

"Life is not all sadness," Old Hawk continued. "Yet, without sadness we would not yearn for joy, and strive to find it, and treasure it when it comes. It is also a fact that neither sadness nor joy is with us constantly. And how often one or the other is part of our journey is not always within our control. We all want joy more than sadness and rare is the person who wants sadness at all."

"I will be happy if I never know sadness ever again," said Jeremy. "But then I know I'm not the first to wish that, and I won't be the last."

"Yes. All of us wish that at one time or another. We wish it because we know there will be sadness," replied the old man. "In part we acknowledge the reality of sadness, and in part we reject it. The reality of the sun shining today does not eliminate the reality of gray skies and rain tomorrow."

"So the reality of joy will not eliminate the reality of sadness," concluded Jeremy. "I think we all know that."

"A simple reality that we often forget," Old Hawk pointed out. "Though one reality may obscure another, it cannot eliminate the other. Perhaps, in the end, the perspective we can gain is that one reality defines another."

"Like losing makes us appreciate winning."

"Of course," said the old man. "Without losing, what would be the worth of winning?"

Old Hawk smiled and pulled a bag of tobacco and packet of cigarette papers from his shirt pocket. Within a minute or two he had finished rolling a cigarette, made with the dried and crushed inner bark of a red willow. Very few people used the red willow bark anymore, or even knew of it. But that was the kind of person the old man was. Old Hawk knew about old things and old ways that others had long forgotten. He lit the cigarette, took a long pull, and slowly blew out smoke as his eyes narrowed and looked across the prairie. Extending a hand, he moved slowly as if painting the horizon in broad strokes.

"When I was a young man," he said, "the last wolf in this part of the country was hunted down and killed. The newcomers to this land brought their long-held fears of the wolf with them. The newcomers thought, and still think, that the wolf was successful because he loved to kill and was good at it. To them, he was evil and had to be killed. They didn't realize that he failed more than he succeeded. He went hungry eight or nine times out of ten because his prey got away. When he finally succeeded the tenth time, he satisfied his hunger. What others saw as a lust for killing was really perseverance. That was the secret of his success: He never quit."

"But the wolf couldn't quit because in his world success meant survival for his family, and failure could lead to starvation and death," Jeremy interrupted. "Failure doesn't always bring such a harsh penalty, for us, I mean."

Old Hawk nodded thoughtfully. "Yes, most of us would agree that there are few penalties for losing harsher than death. For us two-leggeds, losing isn't always so severe. However, losing can weaken our spirit, and dampen our enthusiasm for putting forth effort. We would do well to follow the wolf's example and continue the pursuit of victory no matter the number of failures. As the wolf learned long ago, of the many rewards for winning, two are most important: Victory obscures loss, and it replenishes the spirit.

"And so it goes."

Old Hawk took a long pull on his cigarette before he snuffed it out beneath his heel. For several moments he stared out across the land. And just as the first nibbles of impatience began to bite at Jeremy, the old man turned to him once again.

"Without falling, how would you know when to stand?" he asked.

"Without hunger, how would you learn to appreciate abundance?

"Without bad, how would you measure good?

"Without the finality of death, how would we appreciate life?"

The last question brought a stab of sadness to the young man, but he took a deep breath to stifle a sob and held back his tears.

"Your father has left us," said Old Hawk gently, "because death came through the illness. If you must contemplate the circumstances of his death, then you must also remember how he lived.

"Difficult experiences, whether they are sadness, loss, hunger, poverty, illness, or death, rarely occur because you invited them into your life. But when life does place hardship in your path it *always* offers a chance to learn strength. That is the unseen gift.

"It is not easy, I know, to think of this time and this sadness as a gift. But you can make it so by living through it, one moment at a time, one day at a time. At the end of those moments and those days, you will be stronger. That will be your gift."

Old Hawk discreetly studied his grandson's face. In the young man's eyes he saw a spirit in turmoil. But there were also signs of a mind deep in thought. Patient as ever, the old man lapsed into silence. Finally Jeremy sighed and spoke.

"Grandpa," he said, "I know that denial is usually the first reaction in dealing with sadness and loss. I think I may be doing that."

The old man nodded. "Well," he replied, "the bad will come whether we deny it or not. Good times, easy ways, happiness, and all the positive things we experience are only part of the reality. There is also the negative, the bad times, and difficulties.

"The fact is, the sun does not always shine. Gentle breezes can grow into tornadoes. Too much rain can lead to flood, and too much sunshine causes the drought. Life is life—it is what it is. It offers no certainties, except that it will go on with or without you. The sun will rise and set every day. Though clouds obscure your perception and you do not see it coming up and going down, it will do so nonetheless. So do the seasons follow their unerring cycle, waiting for no one or nothing. The seasons turn into years and the years into ages. Neither waiting nor caring if you join them, but never denying your choice to do so. They will go, and so must you because your journey is waiting. And in your journey you will learn reality and balance."

"Reality and balance?" asked Jeremy.

"Yes. If there is truthfulness, then there are lies. There is generosity—"

"And there is greed," said Jeremy.

Old Hawk smiled. "There is hate," he said.

"And there is love," Jeremy replied.

"There is war."

"And there is peace."

"There is despair."

"And hope."

"There is grief."

"And there is comfort."

"There is defeat."

"And victory."

"There is weariness."

"And rest."

"There is death."

"And there is birth."

Old Hawk nodded his approval. "It is only natural for you to think and to wish, and sometimes even to pray, that the bad things do not happen in your life," he said. "You must learn that the answers to those wishes and prayers have *already* been given to you before you wished and prayed. There *is* love to overcome hate; generosity can diminish greed; truthfulness can reveal the lies in the same way the wind dries the flood and rains end the drought.

"That is life—it is what it is."

Jeremy looked past his grandfather at the vast prairies stretching to the horizons. He sighed and nodded.

■ | ■   *"Life is a journey sometimes walked in light,*
       sometimes in shadow."

"Grandpa," said Jeremy, "why haven't I ever seen you afraid?"

"Because you haven't been looking carefully," replied Old Hawk. "I have been afraid many times in my life. Even now there is a fear that I carry with me. I am afraid of losing your grandmother."

Jeremy was astonished. He had never heard his grandfather admit to any kind of fear. But he had done it so matter-of-factly. "I hope that I can admit my fears as calmly," Jeremy said.

"Many things come with age," Old Hawk assured him. "Your grandmother and I are old. We have been together most of our lives. If she dies first, I would be lost.

"We are all afraid of something. But that shouldn't stop us from going on every day. We should not always walk in fear of the shadow while we are in the light. It is certain we will not know when or how the difficult and bad times will come, but if we accept that they will come, then they are easier to face when they do.

"And always remember that anything that causes the shadow is smaller than the source of the light."

Jeremy looked up at the sun above the rustling leaves of the cottonwood tree. The tree was a giant, but it was infinitely and incomprehensibly smaller than the sun. "Well," he asked, "if the sun is a metaphor for good, are you saying that good things will outweigh the bad?"

Old Hawk shaded his eyes and looked up through the trees. "Sometimes they do, or can," he said. "But the point is we can't always avoid the shadow. My father told me a story about shadows and sunshine when I was young. It's a story of two travelers."

TWO MEN JOURNEYED the length and breadth of a land bathed in sunshine. One was a woodcarver and the other a reader of the law. Their journey was pleasant. The road was wide and there were inns at which they rested for the night. Constables and soldiers frequented the road, so the two travelers knew they were safe from thieves and or anyone else who intended harm. Therefore, though these things were blessings, the journey was without excitement or challenge. After several days the road led into a tall, very dark and thick forest. The reader of the law stopped at the edge of the forest and refused to take another step.

"We must go into the forest," insisted the wood-carver. "It is part of the journey."

"But I do not like the deep shadow," said the reader of the law. "I do not know what could be hiding there in the darkness. There could be thieves ready to fall upon us, or perhaps fierce, wild animals."

"True," replied the woodcarver. "The forest is where many things do dwell. There may be other travelers, or dangerous and unknown things. Yet we will not know until we walk into these shadows. But there is something in there that is the most dangerous of all. That I know."

The fearful reader of the law recoiled. "Whatever do you mean? What can be more dangerous than thieves or wild animals?"

"Your fears," replied the woodcarver, as he entered the forest.

He walked deep into the shadows. More than once he hid from bands of thieves looking for people to rob. Another time he climbed a tree to escape the reach of an angry bear. Before he reached the other side of the forest he had to deviate from the trail to find water, and he became lost. But he managed to find the trail once again and after several days and nights he emerged on the other side of the forest, and found the sunshine again.

The reader of the law, meanwhile, remained at the edge of the forest, afraid to face the shadows.

"What do you suppose happened to that man, the reader of the law," wondered Jeremy. "Did he stay at the edge of the forest?"

"What do you think?" countered Old Hawk.

"Well, I guess sometimes we create our own shadows," reasoned Jeremy. "So maybe he never figured out that his fears made the forest darker than it really was. If so, he could not have learned what the wood-carver did."

"And what did the woodcarver learn?" asked the old man.

Jeremy thought for a moment. "Sometimes we have to endure the darkness, and what it holds. If we do that, we appreciate the light. So the man who wouldn't go into the forest was trying to deny that shadows are a part of life," Jeremy decided.

"True. Furthermore, he gave into his fears and denied himself the experience of facing them," replied the old man. "So he learned the wrong lesson. We all do that from time to time. Instead of worrying how I will face life without your grandmother, I will make the most of the time we have left together, and thank Grandfather for the life he has given us."

TWO

Old Hawk lapsed into another period of silence, but a longer silence than before. Jeremy, however, was familiar with this habit. All elders had a way of using silence to speak for them. And the young man did what was expected of him: He waited.

The leaves continued to rustle and the breeze also stirred the tall grasses nearby. By and by the old man noticed a hawk circling high above the cottonwood tree, and pointed at it. They watched it together until it glided toward the west and became a small speck over the horizon.

Jeremy sighed. "It must be good to know where you are going," he observed. "At least most of the time."

"Well," said the old man, "you and that hawk have much in common."

The young man waited once more.

"What is guiding that hawk?" the old man asked. "Is he riding the wind where it takes him? Or is he following his own will?"

"Perhaps the wind is blowing in the direction the hawk wants to go," suggested Jeremy.

Old Hawk smiled.

"Life is like the wind," he said.

"You did not ask to be born, but you are here."   ■ ❙ ■

"If that hawk does not care where the wind takes him, he is allowing the wind to choose for him," pointed out Old Hawk. "If, as you said, the wind is blowing where the hawk wants to go, then *he* is making the choice. That's what you and the hawk have in common: You are both subject to your own choices."

"But we don't have total control, in spite of that," Jeremy pointed out. "What others do does affect us, or can."

"Indeed. In this journey full of choices, you began your life as a consequence of a choice made by your parents. Where and when you came into this world cannot be changed. The beginning of your journey is carved into the unyielding stone of the past. You should waste no time and effort yearning that it might have been other than what it was.

"What you are comes from the blood of those who set you on this journey. That is likewise unchangeable. What you see in the reflecting pool of truth is who you are. You cannot change that, so it is wise not curse it. The wiser choice is to embrace it and make it your strength.

"Who you will be at the end of your journey is taking form as you travel, molded by the different roads you choose. Those choices, those roads, will add to or take away from who you are becoming.

"And the journey is always perfect no matter what roads you choose. There is a story about choices your grandmother likes to tell."

Two women, no longer young, sat together and talked about the lives they had lived. The first woman had married young and raised several children. She and her husband had worked hard to have a home and provide for their family. They had spent their lives in that home in a valley along a river. Neither of them traveled very far from their valley. As time went by, their children grew and eventually had children of their own. But all the years and years of hard work had finally taken their toll on her husband, and he died.

The second woman, on the other hand, had married a man who was an important official. His duties took him away from home to far and distant places. She frequently traveled with her husband, and therefore saw many different lands and people from different backgrounds. Although her house was filled with treasures from those faraway places, there were no children. Her husband wanted none, afraid they would hamper his career, and she acquiesced.

So as the two women talked, a question arose in each of their minds. Why couldn't things have been different?

It troubled each of them that they might have been able to live a different life, and didn't. Unable to find answers, they decided to speak with a very old woman known for her wisdom and kindness.

The old woman listened to the two women as they told the stories of their lives, and their questions about what might have been. She was not surprised as she listened to them describe their lives, the dreams realized and unfulfilled. When they finished, she reached into a closet and withdrew two woven wool blankets, identically plain and gray. She gave a blanket to each woman. Then she gave them needles and many spools of different-colored thread.

"Decorate your blankets, each of you," the old woman instructed. "When you have finished, bring them to me, and then we will talk again."

The two women were a little puzzled, but they did as the old woman bid them.

Many days later the two women returned with their blankets. Each had decorated one entire side of her blanket. The old woman was pleased.

"Let us look at your blankets," she said, and hung them on a wall.

"Well, well," she chuckled, "just as I thought. Though all I said was to decorate your blankets, each of you has told the story of your life."

Indeed they had.

On the first woman's blanket was a series of scenes, vignettes of her life. First there was a man and a woman, then babies and children, and children grown into adults with babies of their own. A man and a woman tilling the Earth and bringing in the harvest; a house standing near a river in a valley beneath a wide sky. She had used almost every color from the spools of thread; vibrant greens, bright blues, fiery reds, glowing yellows, soothing lavenders, and soft oranges.

The second woman had used the same colors as well, though understandably, the vignettes of her life were different. On her blanket were pictures of trains and ships, and desert lands, mountain ridges, and great cities, and people with various styles of clothing, and animals of different shapes and sizes.

"You came to me and asked if your lives should have been different. I believe you have answered your own question, each of you. Both of your lives could have been different, if you had made other choices; if you had turned left instead of right, if you had said 'no' instead of 'yes.' If the lives you lived were unacceptable and you were truly unhappy with them, you would have told the story of your lives as you wished they could have been. Yet you told them as they were. You could have changed your stories but you did not. Now you can think about the choices you make from this moment on."

The two women took their blankets home, and each of them found a wall in her house to hang them. Every morning each woman awoke and looked at her blanket and faced the day with a smile. Every evening each looked at her blanket, and whispered a prayer of thanksgiving.

And if you were to ever visit them and see their blankets, chances are you would be drawn to the images and the colors, and not notice the blankets were gray underneath.

Jeremy looked at his grandfather's hands, rough and scarred from years of hard work. He couldn't imagine his grandfather being anything other than what he was. He wondered what choices had guided him. How had he ridden the winds?

"Grandpa, do you ever wish your life had been different?" he asked.

Old Hawk chuckled softly. "We all do sometimes. We think 'It ought to have been different,' usually after we've been shamed, or embarrassed, or when we've failed somehow. There are places in the world I wish I could have seen. Places you have seen and described to me, like the Grand Canyon, that mountain in Alaska, Denali, and the oceans you have seen. Yet, at this moment, I am thankful for who and what I am and for how my life has turned out. I have known disappointments, to be sure.

But I have also won the love and loyalty of a fine woman, your grandmother. She was the wind in my life. We were fortunate to have two fine children; your mother and your uncle. Now you, and all our grandchildren, are in our lives. I have been blessed to see my children turn into good, kind, strong, and compassionate people, and now I get to watch you as well.

"I might have wished that things could be different, but I would not change anything of my life. Neither the good nor the bad."

"I hope I don't disappoint you," Jeremy said to his grandfather.

"You won't," the old man reassured him. "Because I know you will try to do what is right and good."

"How can you be so sure?" Jeremy wondered. "Sometimes I don't know what's right and what's wrong."

*"You have weaknesses as well as strengths.
You have both because in life there is two
of everything…"*

Old Hawk gestured up at the tall, old cottonwood towering above them. Its girth was so large that a grown man could not put his arms around it. Old Hawk's father had planted it as a sapling in 1896, the same year he had received an allotment of land from the government.

"This tree," he said, "has stood guard over our family all its life. Strength is what I feel each time I look at it. Yet, there have been moments when its great strength was also its weakness."

"That's hard to believe," Jeremy said. "It's the biggest tree for miles around."

Old Hawk pointed at a thicket of chokecherry shrubs in a dry creek bed not far away. "Look there," he said, "those chokecherry trees are small and weak in comparison to this cottonwood. But when you were a child, they survived a tornado without losing a branch. This old cottonwood, on the other hand, lost several branches. Do you know why?"

"No," replied Jeremy.

"Because, in that instance, the cottonwood's great strength became its greatest weakness. It stood up to the storm, but it could not bend with the wind the way the chokecherry trees could.

"Sometimes we give into our weaknesses, as a young man did a very long time ago…"

OUR PEOPLE WERE STILL living free on the prairies. But there was turmoil because of the growing presence of the newcomers. Many of our people had given in to the authority of the newcomers. One band, however, was still wild and free and living in the region east of the Shining Mountains; the Big Horn Mountains.

During those times of difficulty, one man rose among the people and became a good leader. He was a courageous warrior on the battlefield, and in his village he counseled with his elders and made good decisions on behalf of the people. So, of course, the people came to him because they trusted his judgment, and over the years his village grew.

One day a young man came to the village of this wise leader. The young man's village had been attacked by the newcomers, and many had been killed or captured. All the young man had were the clothes he wore, his weapons, and his horse. He asked the wise leader if he could join him.

The wise leader looked at the destitute young man and said, "We are happy to have you live among us. But first you must do one thing."

"Yes," replied the young man. "Tell me what to do."

"Find the poorest family in the village," the wise leader instructed. "Give your horse to them."

The young man was devastated. He had already lost his friends and relatives, and now he was being asked to give away his most prized possession.

"Uncle," said the young man, "I cannot. Except for the clothes I wear and the weapons I carry, my horse is all I have." Sad and confused, the young man went away.

"Why did you ask that young man to give away his horse?" asked one of the men in the village council.

"Because I wanted him to learn that he could have become part of something larger than his own troubles," replied the wise leader. "We have many horses in our village and I would have given him one from my own herd. But first I wanted to see if he could surrender some of his pain, and make the sacrifice I asked of him. In these times we all must make sacrifices for the good of everyone. Perhaps, after he has thought of it awhile, he will return."

"So," said Jeremy, "that young man's weakness was selfishness."

"Yes," replied Old Hawk. "And if he could have overcome it, he would have received much more than the value of the horse. Not only would he have been given another horse, but the entire village would have embraced him."

"So how do we overcome our weaknesses?" Jeremy asked. "They're as much a part of us as our strengths."

"Sometimes we cannot," said Old Hawk. "Remember, to our people, balance is essential and it should be important to everyone. It is a reality in the natural world. Night and day, life and death, hot and cold, wet and dry, up and down, male and female, and left and right, for example.

"Weakness and strength are necessary for balance. No one or nothing is only weak or only strong. But some of us overlook our weaknesses, and even deny that we have them. That can be dangerous, because denying there is a weakness is in itself a weakness. Likewise, accepting that we have weaknesses becomes a strength. And by the same token, overestimating strength is a weakness. You should not be blinded by your strengths. The feeling of strength is not the same as having strength.

"Neither should you ignore your weaknesses. Know them well, too.

"When all is said and done, accept who you are in the moment you are living. In the end, wisdom is born of weakness as well as strength."

"Within you is the will to win, as well as the willingness to lose…"

Old Hawk looked into the distance over the rolling prairie, and pointed to a small herd of horses galloping across a pasture.

"The one in the lead is a twelve-year-old mare," he pointed out. "She's always in the lead. She doesn't like to lose, even if it's just a lope."

"You're right," Jeremy said. "That mare is a born runner."

"Not only that," the old man replied. "That mare has given birth to several fast runners. The one trying to keep up with her now is one of her foals. She's learning from her mother."

"But horses are born with the ability and instinct to run," Jeremy pointed out.

"You're right. That filly already knows how to run. Her mother is teaching her how to win. We are all like that filly, in a way. At least we all started out the same. Like that filly, you were born with the instinct to succeed. We all were. That is what takes us away from our mothers' embrace, and leads us to the journey that is our life.

"First, that instinct wills you to sit upright so you can see what is all around you. Then it drives you to crawl, pushing you with a sense that you need to move.

"Then you stand because something mysterious tells you there is a wider view from up there. You take your first step, then another because you know you must keep moving. You sense that the journey begins at one place and ends at another.

"Though you fall many times, you rise again and again, stronger and more balanced each time. You are determined so failures do not deter you, and successes only strengthen you. You are encouraged to keep trying.

"But though life beckons it is not a sign that it will always look on you in favor. It beckons because you must make your journey, and you soon learn that in that journey there is also disappointment, failure, sorrow, frustration, weariness, and doubt. Just as you were carried along by your determination, you find yourself dragged down by failure. Then you learn that inside you, along with the will to win is a willingness to lose, to stop when the hill seems too steep, when the road becomes too narrow and rough. That willingness will speak to you of self-pity, and sometimes it will plead, and sometimes rant. But always it tries to make you stop."

"Grandpa, what do you think is the difference between *will* and *willingness*?"

"Well," said Old Hawk, "we inherit the *will* to try and to win. After all, we two-leggeds have survived on this Earth for God knows how long. Untold thousands of generations, I would guess. We didn't survive that long just because we were lucky. Like what that mare passed on to her filly, we get that same spark, that dose of strong will that makes us determined.

"Then life comes along and teaches us how to lose by handing us failures. We learn that quitting is always an option. We learn that it is easier and less painful to simply quit.

"So as a result, a *willingness* to lose creeps in as part of the reality of failure. You are not allotted a certain number of victories in your life, or a certain number of failures; only the knowledge that victories and failures will occur.

"On the other hand, to lose in spite of your best efforts diminishes the willingness to accept defeat.

"Do you remember the story of Long Walker? I think I first told you when you were a little boy."

Jeremy nodded as the story came back to him, just as the breeze made the cottonwood leaves rustle a little louder.

"I don't remember it all, perhaps because of my old age," chuckled Old Hawk. "Maybe you can refresh my memory."

Jeremy cleared his throat, somewhat surprised at the old man's sudden lapse. Then he realized there was a reason his grandfather wanted him to tell the story. "I think I remember it," he said.

L ONG WALKER was one of our people. His name was something else, before the incident. Ah, Red Leaf, I think, because he was born when the leaves were changing colors. In any case, it was nearly winter and the people had settled in along the Great Muddy River, the Missouri. As it turned out, it was one of the worst winters the people could remember. A white man came, a fur trader, on his way back down the river. It wasn't unusual in those days for traders to travel alone in our country. He stayed in the village for a few days and then went on his way. But he brought a sickness to the village; a coughing sickness, probably whooping cough.

A number of people became seriously ill, and some died after several days. The people didn't know what to do because there was no healer among them, and the old women who knew about healing plants could do little against a sickness that was new to them. So the head men decided the best thing to do was send for help. But the best rider among them was one of those who had fallen ill. And though some of the head men had doubts about him, they asked Red Leaf, only because he was one of the few who was not sick. So he agreed to ride north to another village and procure medicine from their healer.

But before he reached that village, a storm came, a real howler of blizzard. But in spite of the snow and cold winds, Red Leaf continued, sometimes leading his horse when the snow became too deep to ride.

He managed to find the other village and told his story to the head men and the healer. So the medicine man performed a ceremony and prepared medicine for Red Leaf to take back—medicine made from the ground leaves of a certain plant.

After only a night's rest Red Leaf started back for his own village, with the medicine in a bag. But the weather only turned worse. Another blizzard howled in from the north with winds so strong that even the buffalo sought shelter in thickets and gullies. Red Leaf couldn't travel for two days. And even after the storm had stopped the snow was so deep that his horse was exhausted just trying to walk in it. To make matters worse the snow had covered the grasses that horses normally dug up to graze. So without feed the poor horse grew weak and began to stumble.

Red Leaf was not about to leave his horse, so he took refuge in a chokecherry thicket and made snowshoes. Fortunately he was also able to find a grove of young cottonwood trees, and stripped the bark for his horse to eat. How horses ever figured out that young cottonwood bark was good feed, I'll never know.

Ordinarily, Red Leaf would have built a shelter and stayed warm while he waited for the weather to improve. But the medicine he had was desperately needed. So he continued on, leading his horse.

Eventually Red Leaf ran out of food and the snow wasn't melting. After days of walking in nearly waist deep snow, Red Leaf collapsed. Tired and weak, he nearly lost consciousness where he lay. But he somehow found the strength to rise and keep going. Several more times he fell, and each time it was more difficult to get back on his feet. Finally all he could do was hold on to his horse's neck rope and let him find the way to the village. They arrived, starving and nearly frozen. Red Leaf slept for nearly two days, but in the meantime the people who had fallen ill were given the medicine. In a few days most of the sick began to recover.

In the spring the village honored Red Leaf with a feast and gave him the new name of Long Walker. That's what I can remember of the story.

"Yes, and so it was," said the old man. "Overall, we think of it as one of our 'hero' stories because he brought back medicine that cured the sick and saved lives. My grandfather, when he was a boy, heard Long Walker himself tell the story. He said that all he wanted to do was go to sleep in the snow, because he was so exhausted. Part of him had given up, but another part of him didn't."

"Not everyone has that kind of grit, Grandpa," Jeremy said.

"Perhaps, but Long Walker taught us all something. We forget that all heroes have moments, a fork in the road, so to speak. One way leads to failure, one to success. If he had given in because he was so worn out, he likely would have frozen to death. If he would have died, then the sick people in his village would have died without the medicine. But because he found a way to get back on his feet, Long Walker taught us that it is better to go until you cannot, which is better than quitting when you know you have the strength for one more step."

*"Within you is the heart to feel compassion
as well as the smallness to be arrogant."*

I T WAS A FEW YEARS after the Council at Long
Meadows, around 1854, that several men departed on
a revenge raid. They were heading for enemy territory
many days south of the Shell River. The Shell was called
the North Platte by the newcomers. Of course hundreds
and hundreds of their wagons traveled west along that
river following a road they called the Oregon Trail. Our
people called it the "Holy Road." But those men learned
about something more important than revenge.

The warriors came to a ridge overlooking the Holy
Road. They wanted to be certain there were no newcomers in their wagons in the river valley. They wanted
to cross the Shell River without being seen, if at all possible. The newcomers had brought terrible diseases with
them that had decimated people from many different
tribes on the prairies. As it turned out, a line of wagons
had just passed. But as they prepared to cross the Shell
River valley, the warriors saw a lone wagon in a grove of
trees. They moved closer and saw a woman with two
small children at what was obviously a fresh grave. The
woman was weeping.

Most of the men in the party were young and wanted
to simply leave the woman and children to their fate.

After all, they were newcomers and their kind was bringing nothing but trouble. The young men felt the woman and her children deserved whatever befell them. But the leader of the warriors was a man of experience, and he knew there was no threat from the woman and children. And he surprised the others when he rode into the thicket. Of course, the woman and her children were not only surprised, they were terrified. All the stories they had been told of "bloodthirsty savages" must have flashed before their eyes at the sight of a mounted warrior. They must have thought they were about to die.

Somehow the warrior leader was able to calm the woman and her children, who had scrambled under their wagon when the other warriors had suddenly appeared. He made tea in their pot and offered it to them. Still, fear was the main emotion. The newcomers were afraid of the warriors, and the warriors were afraid of catching some unspeakable disease. The leader coaxed one of his young companions to cook some fresh meat they had killed earlier. All in all, it must have been a strange meal with both sides watching each other warily. But the evening passed without incident.

The warrior leader surmised that the woman was probably newly widowed, and had been left behind by her people. The next morning he attempted to communicate with her by gestures and by sketching crude pictures on the ground. Hesitantly the woman responded.

With hand signs and sketches, she gave the impression that she wanted to rejoin the line of wagons that had abandoned her.

The warriors conferred. Most were in favor of leaving, but the leader convinced them they should help her before they continued on their trek to the south. Even so, two of the younger men rode away in disgust, and the others stayed. The first thing the remaining warriors did was recover the woman's oxen that had strayed. Never had any of them encountered such slow-moving or stubborn creatures as those oxen. Nevertheless they managed to find four of the animals and the woman hitched them to her wagon. After performing what was obviously a small ceremony at the fresh grave, the woman loaded her children in the wagon and the curious procession started.

Never before, or likely since, had warriors escorted such a wagon and its occupants. An unlikely alliance if there ever was one. Two days later they came within sight of the wagons that had left her, and there the warriors stopped, and the woman went on. The warriors stayed on a hill until they saw that the woman was able to rejoin her people. After that, the warriors took up the revenge trail once more.

Jeremy slowly shook his head. "What happened to those warriors? Did they come back alive from their raid?" he asked.

"One or more of them did, since the story of the woman and her children was told," said the old man. "And there is mention, in some stories here and there, that the leader of the warriors was criticized and ridiculed for helping that woman."

"Why do you suppose he wanted to help her?" Jeremy wondered. "After all, she was one of the people who turned out to be our worst enemies."

"If you think those men, who were like your father and my father and grandfather, were oblivious to her predicament, then maybe part of you also believes the stories that we were 'uncivilized.' I think they helped her because they were the more civilized. Or perhaps because of the values they were taught by their families. Perhaps those values told them that everyone deserves compassion.

"I believe this: We all come into the world unblemished and untainted. At birth each of us is hope and opportunity. Hope that we will keep to the path of goodness, and an opportunity for others to shape us in their image and imbue us with their character.

"But as the reality of our journey takes hold, the path we are given or take shapes us and guides us well, sometimes more so than the blood flowing in our veins.

"As we make our journey, many of us succumb to measuring ourselves and others, by how much worldly goods we have acquired, or can acquire. The false lesson is that he or she who has the most is the best.

"It is true that wealth buys power and influence, but it does not buy morality, or kindness, or compassion. The pursuit of wealth can blind us to the fact that all of us, rich or poor, can be generous with our time, love, kindness, and compassion. Those virtues, and many more, we can all have in unlimited supply.

"Anyone who does not exercise compassion is ignorant of the reality that everyone needs it at some time in life; or we forget that someone has blessed us with compassion at a time when we needed it. That is the smallness of arrogance. It is a disease of the soul. It can be highly contagious. Ignorance is its carrier. It ravages the souls of those who think there is no reality beyond themselves.

"Those who suffer from the smallness of arrogance think that ill fortune is the fault of those who suffer it; that good fortune is a privilege that belongs to them. Whatever path you take, Grandson, do not succumb to arrogance and endanger your soul."

"Within you is the way to face life as well as the fear to turn away from it."

After yet another period of silence, Old Hawk glanced at his grandson. The young man's face was no longer so pinched in pain and confusion. The old man smiled ever so slightly and looked up briefly at the softly rustling leaves.

"Grandson," he said, "You know that, among our people, how we live and conduct ourselves in the year following the death of a loved one is very critical. We believe that how you are and how you behave and handle your emotions during that time is how you will be as a person for the rest of your life. We believe this because we know that all of life doesn't end because one life did. Life goes on. Our family has suffered the loss of your father, and especially at a time like this, we must be centered and strong."

"I know that, Grandpa, but it is not easy," Jeremy confessed.

"That's why I'm glad you came, so I can help in some way. So I can remind you that the journey all of us are making is one of constant learning.

"Something keeps us moving, or whispers to us that we should keep moving, to keep going.

"It is that mysterious, often indefinable force that is Life itself. In the days of our youth it lives mostly in our flesh, and bone, and blood. But in the autumn of our years it leads to knowledge and wisdom.

"That indefinable force that life gives us is the ability to face what it brings on our journey. But if you give in to fear and uncertainty at a time like that, you may become like the young man who became known as the Watcher."

A CERTAIN YOUNG MAN was born with very fair skin, though his brother and sister were the color of rich copper. The boy's mother kept him covered and hardly let him step out of the lodge. Only on cloudy days was he allowed to play in the open. As the years went by he grew to fear the sun.

His fears kept him in the shadows and so no one was surprised that he emerged from his lodge mainly at night. He didn't participate in the life of the village. Though he fell in love with a young woman, he didn't pursue her because she loved to walk on the grassy hillside and play in the cool streams—in the sunlight.

He became known as the man without a face and as he grew old he stayed in the shadows to watch others live their lives. And when people caught him watching, he would duck away out of sight.

After many years he was known simply as the Watcher, and he remains to this day just at the edge of life, simply watching. Perhaps you have caught glimpses of him, ducking away from your glance just when you thought you saw him watching you. He will be forevermore that shadow at the edge of life.

"Facing life does not guarantee success," Old Hawk said. "But giving in to fear and turning away from it does guarantee failure.

"Not to face life is not to gain experience, and not to gain experience limits knowledge. Without knowledge we cannot achieve wisdom.

"To have it all we must face life, no matter what."

THREE

Suddenly the breeze paused, as if life was taking a deep breath, and calm descended over them. The cottonwood tree ceased its song. The young man stared up at the motionless leaves. And he felt the deep and utter silence.

Old Hawk turned his gaze to the grass as the silence persisted. He waited, and in a few moments the breeze returned softly and stirred the leaves once again, coaxing them into silvery whispers.

"The Earth has a heartbeat," Old Hawk said. "In between each beat is silence. That silence is the time when the Earth's life force gathers strength for the next beat. You must learn to do the same. Use the silence to gather yourself."

"Life gives and life takes," the old man said. "Life takes our time, and every day is one day closer to the end of our journey on this Earth. It takes our efforts, our sweat, our best intentions, our noblest ideals, dreams, and sacrifices…and still demands more. Then it throws obstacles in our path, surprises, disappointments, indifference, confusion, doubts, and heartaches.

"Yet life does give us much more than the obvious.

"If we can learn to look back on the difficulties we have known, whether old or new, then we have moved past them, at least in time. That we are looking back at a tough experience from the perspective of the present moment means we have survived it. The experience may have taken a toll, as difficulties do, but whatever our losses may have been, we have survived.

"Survival is victory because we know, or we are reminded, that it is possible. The experience, the difficulty, has taught us, or reminded us, that we can be strong.

"Life can be, and too often is, a series of tough times and tough issues that seem to do nothing more than keep us from achieving satisfaction and finding happiness. And, understandably, we are concerned with whatever we fail to accomplish. Unfortunately, that prevents us from realizing that we may be gaining something else—something more unexpected."

The old man paused and the breeze swirled across the prairie. Several yards from the cottonwood tree a small whirlwind formed and danced over the top of the prairie grasses. Carrying a column of dust, it rose into the air.

Jeremy watched until the dust blended with the blue of the sky. His grandfather had told him many times that someone's spirit often came back in a whirlwind.

"Your father told me a story," Old Hawk said. "He said he heard it overseas when he was in the army."

A VILLAGE SAT NESTLED in a valley far from the hustle and bustle of the world that existed beyond the hills. It had all that its citizens required: a mercantile, a school, a library, a church, and a hospital. Life was good in the village but it moved at a pace all its own. And most of the people who lived there were happy. Now and then, however, a young person would look toward the hills, curious about what lay beyond them.

No one in the village did or said anything to discourage any young person from leaving the village. After all, many of them had felt the same yearnings when they were young. And most that had gone out into the world beyond the hills had come back to the village.

No young person was ever discouraged from leaving, nor encouraged to stay, but only to follow what was truly in their heart. If a young person was about to leave, there was one requirement, one ritual that he or she had to honor.

There was a path leading up from one end of the village to the top of the highest hill. It was a series of steps, and at the end of it was a paved highway that led to a bus stop, and a bus that traveled to the outside world. In order to leave the village, the young person had to climb those steps to the highway.

Most young people who wanted to leave the village thought twice, because they had heard stories that the steps were very difficult to climb, and that some of their predecessors had not made it to the top. Nevertheless, curiosity about the world that lay beyond the hills was a powerful motivator, and some young people chose to climb the steps.

On the morning the young person was to leave, his family led him through the main street of the village, lined with friends and relatives who gave him a rousing send-off. The family then took their young person to the start of the path that led away from the village, and there they said farewell.

"When you reach the top of the hill," the young person was told, "you will find a gift waiting for you."

So the young person began his journey to the outside world by climbing. The stairway was nearly a mile long, made of wood slabs and guarded by a sturdy wooden fence on both sides, so the climber couldn't deviate from the path.

At first the climb was easy because the path was wide, but it gradually became narrower and narrower, and the steps likewise became gradually higher a fraction of an inch at a time. Halfway up was a bench, a place to rest. Here the climber stopped, but only briefly until his heart stopped pounding. Perhaps he was somewhat surprised that he was panting a little.

Further up the hill, he stopped again. His heart was definitely pounding and he was panting harder. At that point he realized that the path was much narrower and the steps higher. And he hoped that the gift waiting at the top was worth the climb.

The rest of the climb was even more difficult. The young person had to stop often to rest. Not only did the path become very narrow and the steps become higher, but the steps were now also very narrow. He had to grab the fence railing on either side to keep from slipping. But he did finish the climb, his heart pounding like a drum, his legs trembling from exertion, his lungs burning. He gained the final level and the gate to the outside world. The highway was only a few yards away.

He looked for the gift but saw nothing, only another wooden bench. There he sat and rested. His parents had told him there would be a gift, but he saw nothing, no object that looked like it might be a surprise. Finally, the bus that would take him to the world beyond the hills arrived, and he boarded with a last glance.

Then he saw it.

Carved into the arch above the gate were the words: STRENGTH IS THE CHILD OF EFFORT AND PAIN.

"What about the people who didn't leave the village and go to the outside world?" asked Jeremy. "Weren't they denied the experience to learn what that young man did?"

"Perhaps," replied Old Hawk. "Then, maybe they learned the same lesson by simply living life. Climbing those stairs is life itself."

*"Strength can come from facing the storms
of life, from knowing loss, feeling sadness
and heartache, from falling into the depths
of grief…"*

"Storms come," said Old Hawk, "it's a fact of life living here on the prairies. Sometimes they surprise us. Other times we can see them forming and we can't help but anticipate what's coming, because we know about storms. Then they hit and we feel their force and ferocity and ride them out the best we can.

"Life is like that, too. Difficult, bad, and downright ugly things can and do happen to us—illness, accidents, poverty, loneliness, betrayal, homelessness, recurring nightmares, death of a parent, a child, a friend, or a spouse. And if that weren't difficult enough, diseases attack our bodies and hearts and minds and spirits. Then old age takes our hair and our dignity.

"Your grandmother is an example of someone who has known many storms in life," the old man reminded Jeremy.

"You mean Grandma Eunice?"

"Yes. She lost her first husband when she was still young. She married again, and the first child she had with her second husband drowned in the river. Then her son from her first marriage was killed overseas during that war in 1967. And now her second husband can't stay away from the alcohol. Yet, what is the first thing you notice about her whenever you see her?"

"She smiles," Jeremy replied without hesitation.

"I don't think there is anyone around here who is emotionally or spiritually stronger than your grandmother Eunice.

"Facing those storms, those unbelievably hard times, means accepting the reality of life. Because denying that bad things can happen never prevents them from happening.

"Life is meant to be lived, not avoided.

"Unfortunately, as Grandma Eunice can tell you, no one ever hands us a manual that tells us what life is all about and how to live it. There are no ten easy lessons, nor even a hundred. But to face every day with its set of experiences and circumstances is fuel for the soul and energy for the spirit, because every day adds to what and who you are.

"You rise every morning with the opportunity to grow, to add to the depth of your character, to increase your knowledge. Every experience, no matter how meaningless it may seem to be, is a gift. And so is every person who crosses your path, whether friend or foe, because difficult situations and difficult people teach us patience and tolerance.

"Positive experiences are also part of the realities of life. It isn't that two or three positive experiences are worth a certain number of bad ones, or anything of the sort. But we can learn that good is reaffirmation of good, and bad can also be good—though it may not seem so at the moment. We can learn that the axiom *whatever doesn't kill you can make you stronger* has a definite ring of truth.

"But the most important word is *can*. Whatever doesn't kill you *can* make you stronger.

"Whether or not you come away stronger, more knowledgeable, or wiser from whatever didn't kill you is not a given. You need to make it work. It needs to be a 'tempering' experience. Do you know what that means?"

Jeremy nodded. "Tempering is that process when red hot iron is immersed in cold water. That immersion strengthens the iron."

"Exactly," said Old Hawk. "Sometimes we are suddenly immersed in a crisis, or an event that—if we use it—can make us stronger. But that tempering process means that it is necessary to deal with the hard facts of disappointment, sadness, and grief. Part of that process is not to deny those feelings. No one embraces disappointment, sadness, or grief, but neither should we deny ourselves the necessity of experiencing the entire array of human emotions. When our spirit tells us it is time to weep, we should weep. It is part of the ritual, if you will, of putting sadness in perspective and gaining control of the situation."

"Well," said Jeremy quietly. "I guess even grief can teach us something."

"Yes, grief has a purpose. Grieving does not mean you are weak. It is the first step toward regaining balance and strength. Grieving is part of the tempering process."

Old Hawk paused for a moment. "How many times have you been in the Rebirth ceremony, the one other people call the sweat lodge?" he asked.

Jeremy shrugged. "Oh, I don't know, maybe two hundred times, or so. Why?"

"As you know, our people believe that the ceremony purges our troubles and problems. We pray for that inside the enclosure during the ceremony. When water is poured over the hot stones and it causes us to sweat profusely, that is the physical and symbolic part of the ceremony. Sweating is purging, and cleansing. Grieving is like that ceremony. It helps purge the sense of loss and anger.

"Facing the storms of life begins with knowing that they will come. We hope and pray that there will be few of them to plague us, but we must expect that they will come. And when they do, we must face them—first and foremost—with our best, meaning who and what we are."

"You must stand up in the storm. You must face the wind and the cold and the darkness…"

"I have seen how different animals behave in a storm," Old Hawk said. "The bison stand facing into the teeth of the wind, whether it's a rainstorm or a blizzard. Horses find a thicket or some kind of windbreak and stand with their tails to the wind. Some birds will put their heads under their wings, and fluff out their feathers. Others, like the grouse, find shelter in the grass or a low thicket. But they all find a way to endure the wind and the cold.

"How we face a storm is important, but so is the fact that we simply try to endure it.

"In the old days our people had a unique way of selecting leaders. They preferred men of experience. It wasn't unusual for them to approach a man and ask him to lead. Today we elect people who promise us they will do something. Those who promise the most are often the ones who really haven't accomplished much to begin with. I prefer the old days. Back then you knew what a man was likely to do because of what he had already done, or been through."

ONE SUCH MAN was called Stands Alone by his friends and relatives. Stands Alone earned that name. He was a stalwart warrior, one of the first to charge and the last to break off from the enemy. He was steady and reliable and never presumed to tell anyone what to do, he simply did what he thought was right. This was during the time after the horse came to us, and before there were too many newcomers.

Stands Alone had a fine family. He and his wife had a son and a daughter, and he was the kind of man who doted on his children. One summer day his young daughter was attacked by a bear. Her injuries were severe and even the village's skilled medicine man could not save her.

Stands Alone and his wife grieved deeply; yet despite her displays of grief, Stands Alone's wife could not be comforted. After the girl was buried, Stands Alone and his family gave away all of their possessions as a sign of mourning—a tradition that is still a custom of our people. So the family impoverished themselves, but soon the people gave them what they needed, including a new lodge. Both Stands Alone and his wife worked hard to replenish what they had given away and to prepare for the Releasing the Spirit ceremony that was to happen one year after the girl's death. And this they did. They prepared a feast and invited the entire village.

But sadly, tragedy was not finished with Stands Alone. The death of their daughter had been too much for his wife, and one day she took her own life. Stands Alone and his son were devastated. Once more they impoverished themselves by giving away everything they owned, including all of their horses. Then Stands Alone took his son and went away from the village. For a year they lived by themselves. During that time, Stands Alone and his son hunted and acquired a few horses. When the anniversary of his wife's death came, Stands Alone returned to the village and prepared a feast. Once again he gave away all his possessions, this time in honor of his wife.

While he had been away, an old leader, long revered and respected, had stepped down from his position. But before he relinquished his position, he advised the people to approach Stands Alone and ask him to be their head man. And so the people did. The old man advised them that anyone who could face adversity the way Stands Alone had would have been strengthened by it. "Strength that comes from adversity does not weaken in the face of adversity," said the old man.

And so it was that Stands Alone became the head man of his village. Not because of the bravery he displayed on the battlefield, or because of the victories and successes in his life, but because of the way he had faced the difficulties that life had thrown in his path.

"I'll bet Stands Alone was probably a good leader," presumed Jeremy.

"Yes he was, because adversity has much to teach us," said Old Hawk. "But in order to learn, we cannot turn away from it. Facing the wind and the cold and the darkness brought by the storms of life is never easy, but it is necessary."

"When the storm blows hard you must stand firm, for it is not trying to knock you down, it is really trying to teach you to be strong."

The young man sat still, staring into the haze just below the horizon. But Old Hawk had seen that distant look many times, worn by people searching for peace and freedom from confusion and pain. His grandson was staring into a place that was neither beyond the horizon nor below it. He was staring inwardly into an amorphous period in his own life.

Old Hawk cleared his throat. "I know that you can understand what Grandmother Eunice felt when she lost her husband and her children," he said. "I know you understand Stands Alone's pain. In a sense, life has knocked you down; though not on purpose, it probably feels that way. Your grandmother and I felt the same way when we lost our eldest child."

After a moment, Jeremy dragged himself back to the present. "What?" he said. "I didn't know you and Grandma had lost a child."

"Yes," said Old Hawk sadly, "your mother's and your uncle's older brother. He was born in the spring and died in the winter when the Spanish flu came. That sickness broke many hearts that time. Your grandmother's and mine among them. Life knocked us down. At that point in our lives it was the worst thing that could have happened. Your grandmother blamed herself for not being a good enough mother. But the reality was, the Spanish flu took the weakest, meaning the very old and the very young. So we held onto each other and got through that bad time. Life knocked us down but we stood up again. When we did, we realized that the birth of that little boy taught us what the bond between a man and a woman can withstand. His death taught us that we can be strong.

"If it is true that strength is the child of effort and pain, then most of us will have the opportunity to learn strength. This time is your opportunity, Grandson. Effort is standing up to the storm. Pain comes from enduring the worst the storm can throw at us. But then so does strength.

"Storms don't last forever, but it nevertheless seems quite the opposite as wind and cold pound us relentlessly. And it does seem that the storm has every intention to knock us down.

"We can yield to the storm by staying down, or we can stand once more and face it, knowing that it will pass.

"Rising to face the storm once again may seem foolish, perhaps even self-destructive. But I like to think that in some corner of our spirit there is a spark of defiance. That may be how storms teach us to be strong, by awakening that spark of defiance.

"Standing up to the storm, no matter how many times it blows us down, should teach us that we don't need to be as powerful as the storm to defy it. We only need to be strong enough to stand. Whether we stand shaking in fear or shaking our fist, as long as we stand, we are strong enough."

FOUR

"When our oldest son died," Old Hawk recalled, "there were many others who suffered the same kind of loss. The Spanish flu came through the northern Plains like a prairie fire. It hit us all, our people and the whites, too. But we all helped each other. We buried our dead and cried together. Your grandmother and I were young, but we somehow had the sense to listen to our parents and grandparents. They told us to live each day and not worry about tomorrow. Yesterday cannot be changed, they told us.

"So we lived one day at a time and each day was a step to that moment when we could think of our son without weeping. We will always feel sadness, but we are stronger for it."

"Being strong means taking one more step toward the top of the hill, no matter how weary you may be."

Jeremy turned at the soft whisper of footsteps and saw Grandma Hawk approaching with a pot of freshly brewed coffee. She poured them each a cup and joined them under the cottonwood tree.

"I have a story," the old woman said. Her hair was snow white and her face was a road map of life. The twinkle in her eyes always made Jeremy feel like he was important.

"As I have told you many, many times," Grandma Hawk began, "your Grandpa is ten years older than me. But what you don't know is that our marriage was arranged."

Jeremy was surprised at that news, and intrigued by his grandmother's enigmatic smile.

"Oh, yes," she went on. "My mother talked to his mother, and they came to an agreement. I had seen your Grandpa around, of course, but I had never spoken to him. The reason for the arrangement was simple, really. I was born when my mother was over forty years old. My father had died in an accident. My mother was afraid that if something happened to her, I would be alone in the world.

"My mother had known your Grandpa since he was young. He had lost his father, too, when he was just a boy. His mother married again but his second father died after several years. Then she became blind, and your Grandpa cared for her. My mother saw how gentle he was, and how strong, too. Those were the reasons she talked to his mother.

"But here is a story."

L ONG AGO a young woman among our people had three very persistent suitors and she couldn't make up her mind which one to choose. So her father devised a plan to test the young men, to determine which one might be worthy of his daughter.

Near the village was a high hill with a long, long slope leading to the top. The father asked each young suitor to run to the top of the hill and down again seven times. But they had to do it on a cold, rainy night. It was not a race, however, and at the top of the hill sat three old men. Each was to count how many times each young man made it to the top.

So one day they began after the rain had been falling for some time and the long slope had become very treacherous. Running in the mud was by no means easy, but the young men tried. By the third time to the top of the hill, each of them was covered in mud from falling, and soaked to the skin. By the fifth time they were all crawling most of the way on their hands and knees. By the sixth and seventh times they were moving on sheer willpower.

They all climbed seven times then reached the bottom of the slope, and it seemed that the issue of who deserved to marry the young girl was still in doubt. The young men collapsed, believing they had done everything the young woman's father had asked of them. But he had one more request.

"Climb the slope one more time," he instructed.

At that, two of the young men became very angry. "I cannot go again," one protested. "I'm too exhausted." The second agreed. Neither could take another step up the hill. The third young man was no less exhausted, but he stood nonetheless. And with all the remaining strength he could muster, he took one more step, and fell on his face.

People who had gathered to watch the contest helped the exhausted young men to their lodges. The next morning they all awoke thinking that they had failed. In the afternoon, the father of the girl sent a messenger to the lodge of the third young man.

The father chose the third young man, because he found the strength of spirit to try, even though all he could do was fall on his face. He knew that the young man who had tried one more time, even though he was physically spent, would have the strength to be a good husband and provider for his daughter.

"My mother told me that story when I asked her why she had chosen your grandfather for me. And I've never regretted that my marriage was arranged. Because, you see, the longer we travel on this journey that is our life, we learn that there is more than one way to be strong. We can be strong of body, mind, and spirit.

"In the days of our youth, however, we put our faith in flesh, blood, and bone. We think strength is going faster, farther, and higher. We solve a problem by overwhelming it, or wearing it down. But there comes a time when we can no longer do that.

"Eventually we learn to our dismay that we cannot go as fast, or as far, or as high. So we learn the value of turning to our intellect, our ability to reason. We attack a problem only after we've studied its various parts. While flesh, blood, and bone cannot sustain strength indefinitely, we discover that knowledge can. Its strength can grow and grow, indefinitely, if need be.

"With a store of knowledge, we begin to reach for wisdom. As it is revealed to us more and more, we realize that we have reached our ultimate strength. Like knowledge, wisdom grows.

"If knowledge is strength of mind, then wisdom is the strength of the soul."

So saying, Grandma Hawk departed, her shoes raising small wisps of dust in the grass.

Old Hawk smiled. "I've never heard that story of the three young suitors," he confessed. "But your grandmother is always full of surprises. She is right, you know, about how strength changes as we travel our journey. But there is something else.

"Whatever our strengths are at any given moment on this journey, or our weaknesses for that matter, they are not a preventative. Challenges will be thrown in our path.

"Whatever the challenges, whatever the obstacles, we must keep our gaze toward the top of the hill. You might ask, why the top of the hill?

"Because life, we say to ourselves, gives us many hills and mountains to climb. Perhaps a part of our mind and spirit knows that up is a greater challenge than down. Therefore we sense that the objective, or the answer, awaits in a high place. To reach that place we will need to lift ourselves, often to a level of effort we have not attained before. But the reward is greater for climbing upward because little or no strength is required to go down."

"Grandpa," asked the young man. "Have you ever quit at anything?"

"Yes, I have, and I've come close to it many times."

Jeremy was surprised. He could not recall a single instance when his grandfather had given up on anything. "Honestly, Grandpa, I can't remember you ever quitting. But if you did, why did you?"

"Weariness," replied the old man forthrightly. "Quitting because we are weary, fatigued, or drained feels as though it is the right thing to do. Weariness whispers to us, telling us, begging us to stop, to quit, to simply give in.

"As at many places along our journey, we reach a moment of choice, as you are now. We must remind ourselves that the choices we have made have brought us to this moment. We must further remind ourselves that quitting, stopping, or giving in is a choice and not mandatory, no matter how seductive the voice of weariness may be.

"We will always serve ourselves best to take one more step, no matter how small or slow or painful it is, or in spite of thinking that all we have is that one last step. We owe it to our journey, and ourselves, to take that one last step—then determine what to do after we have taken it.

"The will, that force, that energy that drove us to crawl and then to stand, and then to take those first shaky steps on this journey is that which has sustained us throughout.

"It is that same will, that same force, that same energy, that unrelenting part of our being that enables us to take one more step."

■│■ *"It means letting the tears flow through the grief…"*

"I think one of the greatest strengths of our people," Old Hawk said, "is our ability to laugh. Sometimes it's the only way to face something that is especially difficult. We laugh at it. By laughing, we diminish it somehow and we can cope with it easier. Laughing lifts our spirits, and grieving cleanses it. And nothing gives voice to grief like weeping, especially the way our women do it.

"My mother told me about two sisters who lived together, after they were both widowed. They grew old together and then one of them fell ill. The younger sister kept vigil at the bedside until death came. Then she wept. From the depths of her soul she grieved, and her wails filled the room. Those in the room found themselves weeping with her.

"Then, after a time, the weeping ceased. Several of the people in the room embraced the grieving woman, wiping away her tears, as she wiped away theirs.

"Something else that my mother said about those sisters stayed with me. They laughed a lot. So I think the younger sister wasn't afraid to weep because she wasn't afraid to laugh, either. Funny thing is, you can laugh so hard that tears come out of your eyes. I think laughter and weeping have to be related, somehow. And they both should have a place in our lives. No one likes to weep, or should I say, no one wants a reason to weep. But we should not be afraid to cry. On the other hand, I think we should find reasons to laugh.

"Your uncle heard a story not long ago, about a group of men who were close friends. They were all practical jokers but cared deeply about each other as well."

ONE DAY the friends decided to establish a "survivor's fund," as they called it. Each year each of them put money in the pot and the intent was that the one who survived all the others would have the money to spend as he wished. So it went. Year after year each man made his contribution, and over the years as they became older, now and then one of them died. Finally, there were only two of them left and they would tease each other about how they would spend the money.

"What would you do if you were the last one?" one asked the other.

The other thought for a moment and said, "I'll tell you later."

As luck would have it, he died before he ever told his friend what he would do with the money.

There was a lavish funeral with a gold inlaid casket and a sumptuous banquet for all who came. Out of respect, the sole survivor waited a few days before he went to the bank to collect his winnings. He couldn't decide whether he would take a trip to an exotic land or buy himself a fishing boat. He would do neither, as it turned out. There was no money in the safety deposit box, only a note from the man who had just died.

The note said: "I've thought about it, and I want the best funeral money can buy."

Jeremy chuckled in spite of himself. "But Grandpa," he said, "isn't it wrong to laugh at death?"

"Why?" replied Old Hawk. "Death laughs at us; why shouldn't we do the same?"

"I remember the story of a chieftain you once told me," said Jeremy. "He took death quite seriously, it would seem."

"Well, let me see if I can remember that story, and then we'll see if he did or not. That story comes from people called the Celts, I think. Here's how it goes."

LONG AGO in a land across the ocean, a warrior chieftain slowly walked the battlefield. Although he and his men had won a great victory, he moved about solemnly. When he came to the body of one of his fallen warriors, he paused there and brushed dirt and debris away from the man's face—then he wept.

At the body of another of his warriors, the chieftain did the same, and at the next. Then he and his remaining warriors carried home their fallen comrades.

As the years passed, more and more warriors followed this chieftain because he was always a good and brave leader. And because he was also a man of good judgment, his losses as a warrior-leader were never many.

Yet it was not only his bravery or good judgment that brought men to him, that compelled them to follow wherever he led.

They followed him because he grieved for every man that fell in battle.

Jeremy reflected on the story for a moment. "Well," he said, "maybe it wasn't so much that he was taking death so seriously. Maybe he was more into honoring his warriors by grieving for them."

"I think you're right," said Old Hawk. "Grieving and letting the tears flow is least of all an acknowledgement of death. It's a way to honor the person who has gone on to the spirit world, and to help those of us who are still here to keep on living."

■ | ■ *"It means to keep looking for the answer, though*
the darkness of despair is all around you."

"There are things other than death that can take away our will to go on," advised the old man. "Like despair, because nothing can cripple us more than the loss of hope. Weariness may, and does, attack our body and mind. But despair takes aim at the soul.

"But I can assure you this: The person who does not give in to despair will not long be deterred by defeat, nor weighed down by the memory of it. I think this is a good time to tell you the story of the two young men who went looking for stones, but found something else as well."

TWO YOUNG MEN journeyed west from the prairies and deep into the high forbidding mountains. They were on a quest to find and obtain the black stone. Others who had made the quest as young men told them which way they must travel.

The black stone was much coveted by many nations, for when fashioned into knives, lance points, and arrowheads, they remained sharp much longer than other kinds of stone. But there was only one mountainside in one range of mountains, north of a land where the Earth itself bubbled and boiled and hot water flew into the sky. That mountainside was deep inside the territory of a nation unknown to the people of the prairies. Not all the young men who had traveled before in search of the black stone returned. It was a very dangerous journey.

"There is much more danger waiting than enemies, two-legged or four-legged," an elder warned the young men on the eve of their departure.

The young men, who were brothers, were puzzled by the elder's words as they began their journey.

Within a month they reached the mountains. Summer was nearly gone when they found the mountainside of the black stone. They were very adept at hiding and they had moved like shadows across the prairies and in the forests of the mountains.

Each of the brothers gathered a bag full of the black stones. Then they made a secluded camp to rest, and prepare for their journey home. But the trouble they had so adeptly eluded on the journey to the mountains was waiting for them on the way home.

First it came as a giant of a bear that appeared suddenly on a mountain trail. The brothers' only course was to race down the mountain. They managed to escape, but not before the younger brother lost his bag of stones and his weapons. Then came a flash flood. After days of rain forced the brothers to seek shelter, a narrow mountain stream became a seething torrent. They had to climb a tall pine tree to escape the sudden flood.

When they finally came out of the mountains, summer was over and autumn had come swiftly. Overhead the great gray and white geese of the north were flying south.

One day while they were hunting, the brothers were spotted by warriors of an enemy nation. Their only recourse was to flee from the enemy who greatly outnumbered them. But after days of keeping a relentless pace, they were exhausted as well as weak from hunger. Autumn sent cold winds earlier than usual and the nights were bone-chillingly cold. Sometimes the brothers were fortunate to find a cave or a hollow log to sleep in at night, but mostly they were exposed to the unyielding elements.

Nevertheless they kept going and, after several days of running until their moccasins were worn to shreds, they finally eluded the enemy.

One afternoon, however, as they stopped to rest, the older brother pointed back to the west. "Someone is following," he said.

Though the younger brother looked and looked again, he could see no one. But he believed his brother, who had never lied to him.

"We must hurry away," said the older brother. "See! There! He is coming after us!"

Try as he might, the younger brother could see nothing. The two resumed their trek home, anxious for the comfort of their own lodges and of seeing their families. Though they were strong and robust young men, the days without food and rest had taken a toll. They could not run far before they needed to rest.

"There!" the older brother shouted. "He is closer! We must flee before he catches us!"

Though he saw nothing, the younger brother followed, alarmed by the fear on his brother's face. He had never known his brother to give in to fear before.

In spite of sheer exhaustion, the brothers stumbled and ran until they could run no more, finally collapsing during the night. The older brother curled himself into a ball behind a tree, and whimpered.

"He is still coming! Listen!"

He was so beset with fear that he begged his brother not to build a fire, though they needed to warm themselves.

"He will see us!" he whined.

Every sound from the darkness sent the older brother into another spasm of whimpering and hiding. He grabbed stones and sticks and threw them at the enemy that he said was hiding in the darkness.

Exhaustion lulled them both to sleep briefly, but as the sun rose the older brother let out a cry.

"Look! He has grown; he is larger!"

The younger brother had to call on every ounce of strength to keep up with the fear-induced pace his brother set. Finally, though the older brother collapsed and could not regain his feet, he crawled on, whimpering in fear as he went. Soon his hands and knees were cut and bleeding. But always and frequently he glanced back, terror twisting his features each time.

Yet the younger brother saw nothing.

After days of terror-stricken flight, even fear could no longer induce the older brother to move. His body trembled as he lay in a disheveled heap, looking up at an unspeakable enemy only he could see. His trembling fingers pointed, even as his eyes rolled and he fainted from exhaustion.

"He will kill us both!" he warned. "He is a giant!"

The younger brother, not far from blacking out himself, rubbed his eyes and tried to see his brother's giant.

"There!" cried the older brother, pointing at a particular spot.

When the younger brother turned, he saw a shadowy form approaching. But it was not a giant, yet it was something to fear, he sensed. He was about to step back in retreat, but instead something inside made him stumble forward to meet the shadowy figure. Something that told him that the shadow could grow into a giant.

"No!" he yelled. "Go away! I know what you are! Go away!" Reaching into the bag, he grabbed stone after stone and threw it at the shadowy form. Each time he threw a stone, the form grew smaller. Slowly, the form faded until it was no more. But the young man had thrown all of the black stones. Though he did recover a few, he knew the people in the village would be disappointed with them for losing most of them.

On weary legs the younger brother stumbled as he gathered wood for a fire. Only with great effort could he bring his hands and fingers to build a fire starter, and finally to blow the tiniest of embers into wavering little flames.

When the fire burned steadily, he dragged his brother closer to it and built a wall of wood behind him to reflect the welcome heat. Then he too gave in to sleep. He knew what had been chasing them, but he also knew it would not come back.

When the younger brother awoke, the day had passed into night. Only glowing embers remained of the fire. He added wood and coaxed it back to life. He kept vigil through the night, banking the fire to keep them warm. When dawn came, he found a stream and drank to chase away some of his thirst.

Fortunately, the brothers were back in their own territory. They rested at their camp for several days, the older brother sleeping fitfully. The younger brother managed to snare a rabbit and roasted it. That little bit of food revived him.

On an afternoon the older brother awoke with a start, jumping to his feet, his eyes wild and filled with fear.

"The giant is gone," said the younger brother. "He went away. I drove him away."

"How do you know?" asked the older brother, still very fearful.

"The giant came because our fear created him," the younger brother said. "We created him."

"But how did you drive him away?" asked the older brother.

"I threw the black stones at him, each time hoping he would go away, and he did. Now, here is some meat. I will hunt again for more, and we will eat and grow strong again. Then we will finish our journey."

And so they did, reaching home after nearly two months. After resting for several days the two brothers went to the lodge of the elder and told him their story, and presented the handful of black stones they had managed to save. They were ready to be chastised for failing.

"The black stone is good to have. But the true reward for the journey is not a bag full of stones," the elder said. "Because what you saw out there is something that waits for us all anywhere along a difficult road. And life is a difficult road."

"Despair," said the younger brother. "What we saw was despair. But how did it know where to find us?"

"Because it dwells within us," replied the elder. "Not in a place but in a moment when our spirits are weakened because circumstances seem hopeless. Then it appears."

"Then what is the reward, if it is not the stones?" the older brother wanted to know.

"Despair may dwell within us," said the elder, "but so does hope, the way to defeat it. You learned that hope can defeat despair. That is the true reward."

*"Being strong means to cling to hope for one
         more heartbeat, one more sunrise…"*

"We all reach moments in our lives like the brothers did,"
said Old Hawk. "But remember, in the silence after one
heartbeat, life gathers itself for the next beat. So the time
to hope is when despair grabs us by the throat. That is
when we gather ourselves."

"Why should we do that?" Jeremy asked.

"Because hope is one of the sparks by which life sus-
tains itself," replied Old Hawk. "The ability to hope is
one of life's greatest gifts. The moment we hope that all
will end well, that we can accomplish what we set out to
do, we have likely insured that we will gain the outcome
we hope for. At the very least we have increased the odds
in our favor.

"Hope is not available exclusively to any one person.
It is ours to use no matter what our station in life. The
slave hopes for freedom and the rich man for happiness.
But hope is most often the companion of the down-
trodden. It dwells in the hearts and minds of those who
have experienced loss or tragedy, or anyone whose road
seems more uphill than level. In other words, we have all
been in a place or a situation where we have had to hope
for shelter from the cold, for freedom from pain, the

lifting of a burden, or one more opportunity, one more chance to right a wrong.

"There are no guarantees that hope will bring the desired outcome. Every slave may not gain freedom, and every rich man will not achieve happiness. But if we do not or cannot hope we have empowered the cause of our difficulty.

"The older brother in the story of the stones was ready to curl up into a ball and quit. But the younger brother found that spark. Each of us is like those brothers. Part of us gives in to despair but another part of us finds that spark.

"Cling to hope, Grandson, no matter what happens. Remind yourself that there will be another sunrise, and chances are, hope will help you to see it."

▪ ┃ *▪*   *"Each step, no matter how difficult, is one more step closer to the top of the hill…"*

Old Hawk pointed to the top of a small butte that rose from the floor of the prairie. "How many steps would it take you to reach that butte?" he asked his grandson.

The younger man tried to gauge the distance, and finally shook his head. "I don't know, Grandpa, thousands, maybe," he said.

"Perhaps it's not the number of steps that is most important," suggested the old man. "Perhaps it is more important to take the steps. On the other hand, which is more important: the first step that sets you toward that hill, or that last one that gains the top?"

"Well," said Jeremy, "you always said it's important to finish what you start. So that would make both the first and the last steps equally as critical."

"Maybe," allowed the old man, "but it would seem there is more to the journey than the first and the last step. Don't you think? What about the steps in between? And what about the 'next step'?"

"The 'next step'? What do you mean?" Jeremy asked.

"Let's say, for the sake of argument, that it takes you ten thousand steps to reach the top of that hill. But if you make longer strides, it would take less than that. If you took shorter steps, it would take more."

"What are you getting at, Grandpa?"

"What is more important? The length of your stride—how long or how short—or the number of steps? Or maybe it's more important that you simply take the steps, one after another." The old man paused and waited as his grandson pondered for a moment.

"I think it's more important to continue to take one step after another, no matter how long or how short they are," Jeremy decided.

"That's exactly how we get anywhere, whether we travel across the land or toward a goal we want to reach," affirmed Old Hawk. "That's how hope works. It induces effort, it can even coax it from us. Hope can will us to lean forward and take one more step.

"That one more step will take us beyond where we were, somewhere, anywhere, ahead whether by a hairs-breadth or an arm's length does not matter.

"It isn't always necessary to overwhelm a problem or overcome an obstacle in one fell swoop. A series of small victories, small steps, will serve the same purpose. We do not have to gain the top of the hill in one swift leap, or a prescribed number of steps for that matter. All we need to do is reach the top one way or another.

"Hope is always one more step, or one more stone. I read a story some years ago."

THERE WAS A VILLAGE across the ocean nestled in some foothills along a river. The people in the valley prospered from a partnership with the neighboring farmers. They grew wheat in abundance, which was ground into flour by the village's flour mill. The mill's grindstone was powered by the river, which turned the wheel that turned the stone. Then the villagers and farmers sold their flour to merchants across the land.

One spring the rains fell more frequently than usual, and the residents of the village saw the river rising gradually. If the rain didn't stop, the river would flood the wheat fields, and there would be no wheat to grind and sell.

The village council and the farms and all the people in the valley watched helplessly as the river rose higher and higher as the rains continued to fall. The village meeting hall was filled with many people from the valley who gathered to talk about the impending flood. All the farmers were afraid for their livelihood, and many of the valley's residents were afraid that everyone would lose their homes if the rains didn't stop. Everyone in the meeting hall wanted immediate answers from the village council.

In the middle of the spirited discussion, a very old woman with snowy white hair entered and walked slowly to the front of the room. Though simply dressed, she had a very striking appearance, but that was not what drew every eye in the room to her. It was the large stone she carried in her arms.

No one had ever seen the old woman before, and everyone wondered why she was carrying a large stone. Utter silence descended. When she spoke, her gentle voice filled every corner of the room.

"Many live in this valley," she began. "If every person walked to the foothills and brought back the largest stone he or she could lift, perhaps we could divert the flood. Line the riverbank with stones at the lowest spot, as high as possible."

So saying, the white-haired old woman left the meeting hall and took her stone and placed it along the riverbank. Thereafter, she departed into the high country.

Some of the people scoffed at the old woman. Some, however, saw the logic in her words. Soon people headed for the foothills to bring stones to the river. Old and young, weak or strong, the people trekked in long lines, many going more than once to bring back stones. But others were not so certain piling stones was the answer, so they went to their homes and packed their belongings, preparing to flee before the river rose above its banks. By sunset many people were leaving the valley. And those who took the old woman's advice continued to haul stones, carrying them by hand or in carts and wagons.

The lowest spot along the river became a dike made of hundreds, and then thousands, of stones.

The rains persisted and the river rose slowly, pushing and dashing against the stones. As the rains fell harder and harder, some of the people quit hauling stones and fled as others had before. Yet a steadfast few worked even harder to build the dike, hauling as many stones as they could from the foothills. In spite of their heroic efforts, the dike was not quite high enough to hold back all of the water, yet it did hold back enough of the flood. Although some of the fields were flooded and the water reached the edge of the village, most of the wheat fields were saved, and so were many homes. By and by the rains stopped and the river rose no more.

The village council wanted to thank the old woman for her advice. Strangely, however, the messengers they sent into the high country could not find her. She was never seen again.

To commemorate their reprieve from the flood, the people decided to leave the dike made of stones as it was. Some wanted to improve it and make it stronger. Who knew when the rains would again fill the river, they said. But so that they should never forget how they saved themselves from disaster, they built a monument in the village square. It was a simple structure, nothing more than a large log placed upright.

Into the side of the log was carved the face of an old woman. Atop the log was a single stone from the dike.

Jeremy nodded. He had read the story, too. "That stone on top of the log represented hope," he recalled.

"Of course," said Old Hawk. "One stone could not have stopped the river from flooding the valley. But many, many stones could. Yet it did begin with one stone.

"Hope works the same way. One stone at a time, one step at a time, no matter how small or large the stone, or how easy or difficult the step."

"But not everyone in that village pitched in and helped. Many of them fled," Jeremy reminded Old Hawk. "Are we to assume they saw no hope in fighting the flood?"

"Perhaps," replied the old man, "I think there is a place between hope and hopelessness. We can go either way. Those who ran saw it as the only way to save themselves. Those who stayed and built the dike saw it as a way to save everything. But there will always be those of us who will succumb to hopelessness, and those who act on hope. I like to believe that most of the time hope will make a difference."

"To keep hope alive for one more heartbeat at a time leads to the light of the next sunrise, and the promise of a new day."

"Sooner, rather than later," Old Hawk began, "we all learn that life is not easy."

Jeremy concurred silently. Before his father had died, there had been other struggles. He was still paying off student loans from college, and though he wanted to apply to graduate school, he wasn't sure he could pay for two more years of school. A high school in Alaska had recruited him to teach there and the pay was nearly double his current salary. But the cost of living up there was higher, and he wasn't sure he wanted to be so far from home and his grandparents.

"On the other hand," the old man went on, "if our journey has not known struggle and we have experienced little or no obstacles, then whatever we have gained may not be seem worthwhile to us, be it riches, or status, or title, or anything else. If we have not known struggle, then neither have we learned the value of hope.

"Since the world began, the sun has been rising and setting with regularity, a certainty we can depend on. Yet no one on this Earth knows how many more days will come. All we really need to know, however, is that each day can be a new opportunity. What we do with it is up to each of us.

"Yet, time can be a burden or a gift, as your cousin learned after he came home from overseas.

"He had survived the unfettered violence of combat and witnessed the ugliness and inhumanity of war, and wondered—almost every minute of every day—why he was alive and some of his fellow soldiers had died. Not only did he carry an enormous guilt, he questioned the validity of the values he had been taught as a child, especially those having to do with the sanctity of human life.

"He was constantly bombarded with memories triggered by the smells, sounds, and images of war. At night he was terrified of going to sleep because of the vivid dreams of combat. Alcohol became a haven because it numbed his guilt and sometimes softened the jagged edges of his memories and dreams.

"After months of guilt, pain, and despair, he considered ending his life. But in the middle of one night he awakened from a drunken stupor on his parents' floor, with no indication of how he had gotten there. Seated next to him on the floor was his mother, your uncle's wife. She held a damp cloth and was gently wiping the sweat from his face. Her soft touch finally broke the wall of anger and denial the young man had built, and he wept. Through the tears he confessed that he could no longer face the images that were the memories of his buddies.

"When your cousin had cried until there were no more tears, his mother took his face in her hands and spoke.

" 'Do not turn from their faces. Let them come into your mind. Hold them in your heart. They were your friends, your fellow warriors. All of you shared something, whether it was good, bad, or unspeakable. No matter how my heart aches for you, I can never know what you witnessed or endured. They come to you because you may be the only connection they have left to this world. Tell them how difficult it is for you now; they will understand. Then live your life for them as well as for yourself. Honor the gift you have been given, a gift they would take in a heartbeat.'

" 'There is nothing you can do to change yesterday, but you might make tomorrow easier by living the best you can today. When the sun comes up, stand up, square your shoulders and face what comes. You won't have to face it alone. Your friends will be with you every step of the way.'

"In the days, weeks, and months after that night, your cousin remembered his mother's words often. And he took her advice. He let go of the day that had passed each night as he lay down to rest, and didn't worry what the next would bring. The best he could do was hope and pray for the strength to live it well when it came.

"The road was not easy, but he did know where he was going. Then he realized one night as he was about to drift off to sleep, that—for the first time in years—he was eager for the next day to come. After that moment he regarded each day as a promise that there were always possibilities.

"Possibilities, he told me one day, were the children of hope. And your cousin also said that his mom taught him how to hope. She taught him that each new day was worth living for.

"I think she taught him something else. I think she taught him that keeping hope alive is to know how to keep going."

FIVE

Jeremy suddenly realized that most of an afternoon had passed. The sun was well into the western half of the sky. Yet time, at least for this day, didn't seem very important. A large part of him wished fervently that this day could go on and on, so that he could spend the rest of his days in the shade of the old cottonwood with his grandfather.

But even as he wished it, he knew that beyond the shade of the cottonwood his journey awaited.

Sensing Jeremy's mood, Old Hawk leaned forward and squeezed his grandson's knee.

"Life is out there, waiting," he said gently. "I envy you because you will experience things I couldn't. The knowledge you will gain will be greater than mine."

"I don't see how that's possible, Grandpa," protested the young man.

"Oh, but it is, simply because we all stand on the shoulders of those who have gone before us. I know things my father and my grandfather didn't, because they gave me a foundation to step from. And the world has changed since they walked this Earth. That doesn't mean I'm wiser than they were. The best I can hope for is to someday be just as wise. That is the journey I look forward to."

"Was my father a wise man?" Jeremy asked.

"Yes," Old Hawk replied. "Your father was wise, and he was physically and mentally tough. He was a deep thinker, and very spiritual as well. Your father was many things to many people. But I will always remember him for his stubbornness."

"His stubbornness? Why that, of all things?"

"Because of the promise he made to your mother, and kept."

Jeremy felt a lump in his throat. Yes, the promise. Recent memories overtook him.

Two months before Jeremy Sr.'s death, Jeremy and his mother had been told that he could go at any time. It was a conversation that was supposedly out of the elder man's earshot. But he had heard.

Instead of being discouraged or angered by the news, he had uttered a simple promise.

"Don't worry," he said to Jeremy's mother. "I will make it to our wedding anniversary."

Everyone had smiled gamely and nodded, but all knew that it was likely impossible. Their wedding anniversary was four months away.

Jeremy Sr. surprised everyone by hanging on for three more months, but in that time he had deteriorated into a ninety-pound skeleton. Relatives came to the house to spend a few minutes or a few hours; family was always nearby. Everyone was convinced that the days were numbered on the short side. Nevertheless, Jeremy Sr. steadfastly hung on in spite of the pain that medication couldn't always eliminate or even diminish.

His quiet promise had been the cause for many a sad, teary eye, because of the odds against facing each day after pain-wracked day for four months. But on the eve of the anniversary the house was filled with relatives and friends.

Just past midnight Jeremy watched as his mother leaned over the bed and whispered into his father's ear. Though her words were meant for his father only, Jeremy would never forget them.

"Happy anniversary," she whispered. "I love you."

Jeremy saw clarity in his father's eyes, as if the pain had gone away if but for a moment. Then the man nodded, smiled, and closed his eyes for the last time.

"I shudder to think of the amount of pain Dad endured every day," Jeremy admitted. "I don't think I could do that. Maybe it was his stubbornness that carried him on."

"I don't think it was only a physical struggle," said Old Hawk. "If it had been only on that level, your father would not have made it to his anniversary. I think, at some point, his spirit took over, perhaps prompted by his stubbornness.

"You were a long-distance runner in high school. I know there were probably many times you thought you couldn't take another stride because your legs felt like logs. What happened at that moment when your muscles were screaming for you to stop?"

Jeremy thought for a moment, remembering races he had run, and some he had managed to win. "Oh," he murmured, "at a certain point, something else takes over. You find a certain kind of strength, but it's different than physical strength, I think. You somehow rise above the pain and your lungs burning for air, and you keep going."

"Isn't that what your father did?" Old Hawk asked.

"Well." Jeremy sighed. "What my father did was so much more than that. There's no comparison."

"Perhaps," admitted the old man, "but maybe you do have some insight into what he did, and how."

Jeremy nodded as he distinctly heard his father's soft-spoken promise in his head. After a moment he sat up a little straighter.

*"The weakest step toward the top of the hill,
toward sunrise, toward hope, is stronger
than the fiercest storm."*

The rustling cottonwood leaves seemed to sigh as Jeremy wiped away a tear.

"In the last days of his life, your father was still trying to teach you," pointed out the old man. "He was teaching us all. I have seen few people show such courage and grace in the face of pain. Your father wasn't afraid to die, but he was afraid of the pain. Yet he faced it day after day because he made that promise.

"And by keeping his promise to your mother, he showed us how to be strong no matter how weak we are, or think we are. Even in his weakened condition, he kept death at bay. He wasn't trying to cheat death, he was simply keeping a promise and in doing so he became stronger than death, for a time.

"When we find ourselves overwhelmed by a situation, we too often think that small effort is the same as no effort. We don't realize that the difference between a small effort and no effort can be gigantic. It may be the difference between winning and losing.

"Lack of effort, doing nothing, accomplishes nothing. It is the absence of hope, and it empowers the problem. Lack of effort is also self-betrayal. When we do nothing, we become our own worst enemy. If we do not take a step, if we do not make that effort, we are dropping victory into the jaws of defeat.

"Therefore, no matter how useless we think it would be in the face of overwhelming odds to take one more step, we must. The least that can happen is that seemingly useless effort can inspire yet another step.

"And if we can take one step, no matter how slow or no matter how small, chances are we can take another.

"Eventually one of those steps will make the difference, because victory, more often than not, is achieved by a series of small actions.

"Remember the people in the mountain village, and their stone dike. The dike represents the combined efforts put forth by those people who acted on hope. So each stone was one small step, and it led to another, so each stone defeated the flood.

"Life is a journey made one step at a time, sometimes easy and too often difficult. We must make this journey by taking those steps. After all, it begins with a single one. Nowhere is it written that a step must be a certain length to matter or to advance us along our path. Nor is it written that our steps must always be strong. Life simply demands that we take one step at a time.

"Sometimes we are strong and we can make long and purposeful strides. Sometimes the road itself is so rough that all we can manage is a crawl, no matter how strong or weak we are. And as we all know, the journey itself can and does wear us down. Yet we are never diminished or set back, no matter how small, seemingly weak, or inconsequential a step may be.

"Every difficulty, every storm, no matter how large or however strong it may be, can never defeat even the weakest step, because it is an expression of hope. Every step is a prayer answered. Every step is a spark that defies the darkness of despair.

"Defy the darkness."

SIX

Old Hawk pointed to the shadow of the cottonwood tree stretching across the grass. "The sun's journey this day is nearing its end," he observed. "It's been a good day. I wish it not to end, but tomorrow is another day."

Jeremy looked at the long shadow. It was an irrefutable sign that the day was quickly passing. In his mind a myriad of images born of his grandfather's words and stories swirled like leaves in a whirlwind.

"We will talk again soon," promised Old Hawk. "Until that time keep this day in your heart and we can talk anytime and at any point in the journey that waits for you. But you must allow an old man a few thoughts to end this day."

Jeremy smiled and waited.

■ **|** ■ *"Keep going."*

"A river begins its journey quietly as a small stream, usually in some obscure place. But it is a seeker determined to find its way. It does not know how to yield to obstacles, which can deter it for a time but cannot stop it. In a good season a river grows and gathers strength from melting mountain snows. Spring and summer rains also send down their encouragement. However, a bad season with less snow and rain may slow its flow to a mere trickle at times.

"Nevertheless, the river inexorably follows the path it has made for itself, or it carves a new course if necessary. It is unstoppable.

"A river can be wide or narrow, shallow or deep, swift or slow. But of all its characteristics, two are most distinctive: It creates its own path, and it flows relentlessly. So long as there is winter snow in the mountains, spring rains, and gravity, rivers will flow, they will persevere."

The old man paused, then spoke again.

"Rivers are not the only examples of determination in the world around us. There are many, at more than one level of reality. Like the seasons of the year.

"Many human cultures believe that the annual cycle begins with spring, the season of rebirth. Living things renew themselves and life goes on. So do the seasons. Summer follows spring, then autumn, then winter.

"Awareness of this cycle is inherently within all of us, no matter who or what we are. We honor the cycle with all manner of endeavors and rituals. But we seem to be less aware that the seasons never end. They come and they go, endlessly. Perhaps we take their endless cycle for granted, when we could acknowledge it as a testament to perseverance.

"The bison honored the seasonal cycle. There was a time, only a few generations past, when our lands here shook beneath their hooves. No one knows how many there were. It's enough to say the herds were so vast they often covered the land from horizon to horizon. They were literally the source of life for many indigenous human societies of the Plains."

Two HUNDRED YEARS AGO on those very plains, a group of hunters stood on a hill above the confluence of two rivers north of here, the White Earth and the Smoking Earth rivers. For most of a day they had been watching two great herds of bison traveling in opposite directions. One herd was moving to the southwest, the other to the southeast. Both were long, wide columns of darkness against the light grasses of autumn.

The two herds would meet near the river, the hunters surmised. There, they expected, would surely be a scene of mass confusion such as they had never seen. So they waited to see what would happen.

Slowly the herds came, one from the west and the other from the east. And as the hunters had expected, the two herds met just north of the river. However, much to the surprise of the hunters, the two great columns passed through each other. They intersected without deviating. From their vantage on the hill, the hunters saw that each herd kept to its path. There was no confusion. At the river the great animals paused for a drink and then moved on.

The hunters were astonished. By the time the sun had set, the two herds kept going on their separate paths.

When all is said and done, perhaps the secret of life is perseverance.

Like the river, the seasons cycle and recycle, and they keep on going. Just like the two herds of bison.

"Life keeps going," said Old Hawk. "It can be contrary, however. It provides us a journey as well as the many reasons to make the journey—success, power, fame, influence, wealth, satisfaction, purpose—and then throws obstacles and challenges in our way to make us fail.

"We didn't begin our journey with a prescribed amount of failures and successes as a way to let us know when we've reached the end. But many of us do think, or we are tricked into thinking, that after a certain number of successes or a certain number failures, our journey should end.

"Life, we think, measures us by how well we've succeeded or how miserably we have failed," Old Hawk continued. "On the other hand, perhaps life doesn't measure us at all, at least not in the same ways we measure ourselves. Perhaps it doesn't expect us to succeed or fail. Life may simply want us to make the journey in order to add to or detract from the whole. To put it another way, when we reach the end of the journey that is each of our lives, we will be examples to those who come behind us. Some of us, unfortunately but perhaps necessarily, will be examples of how *not to* live life. Others of us will be examples of how *to* live life."

The old man reached for his bag of red willow bark and rolling papers and fashioned another cigarette. After he took the first pull, his eyes narrowed once more as he gazed into the distance. But the young man knew that his grandfather was looking into a place he had yet to see. Old Hawk turned to Jeremy.

"We will end this day with one last story."

IN THE BOWL OF A WIDE and beautiful valley between two spectacular mountain ranges is a village. In it are many kinds of people following various pursuits: There are farmers, hunters, scholars, builders, philosophers, teachers, healers, herbalists, and craftspeople of many different skills. The village is known far and wide for its architecture. Its residences and public buildings are among the most beautiful anywhere.

Yet along the main highway entering the village is a large sign welcoming travelers. A stonemason's mallet and chisel are painted on the sign. To know the story of the mallet and chisel is to know the value of perseverance.

One summer, many, many years ago when the village was still small, a young man climbed the highest mountain peak overlooking the valley and the village. Upon descending he described the breathtaking view he had seen from the peak. It was inspiring to see their village from the perspective of an eagle, he reported. So, of course, everyone wanted to see the village from the highest peak.

But the climb to the peak was very treacherous. Several people slipped and fell, and some were killed. Eventually, no one attempted the climb anymore. So to satisfy everyone's curiosity, the young man who had made the climb sketched a picture of what he had seen. But he was not an artist and his sketch was more frustrating than enlightening.

One day a stonemason had an idea. A series of steps could be carved from the granite of the mountain slopes, he suggested, leading to the top of the high peak. Most people scoffed at the man, however, pointing out that such an undertaking would never be completed in their lifetimes. Undaunted, nonetheless, the stonemason began carving the first step.

The height of the step was half the height of a man, and just as wide and as deep. He finished it after nearly a year. All of his spare time was devoted to carving more steps on the mountain slope with hammer and chisel. But he could work only in the summer and autumn and even then only when the weather was good. So progress on the steps was very, very slow. In ten years he had finished only three steps.

The mason had been past middle age when he started on the steps. By the time he completed work on the fourth step, he was an old man. Many in the village thought the foolishness would end when the mason died. They were astonished when another, younger man took up the task. So the work on the steps continued, but with no less ridicule from the people of the village. There was no support of any kind.

By the time the younger mason finished several more steps, he was past middle age. The villagers were utterly astonished when another man stepped forward to continue the work. Like the two before him, the new mason worked alone.

Most people in the village ignored the mason and the steps. No one spoke to him and he had a difficult time obtaining regular work. He was forced to travel to other villages to work for wages. But he didn't abandon the steps.

In time, new machines—automobiles—appeared in the valley. Horses and horse-drawn buggies, carriages, wagons, and manual farm implements slowly became obsolete. Next the village took down its lanterns from the light poles along the streets and new ones, brighter lamps lit by electricity, were installed. As the years passed, all types of new technological advances came to the valley.

But the work on the steps up the mountainside continued, undeterred and unaided. Most perplexing to the villagers was the succession of stone workers. A new mason always replaced the previous one. Work on the steps continued without aid or interference from the people in the village. Now and then it was the topic of spirited discussions in the village shops and cafés. So, too, were the stone workers who carved the granite of the mountain to shape the steps. One had been affable enough, but the others were not inclined to associate with the villagers, except when it was absolutely necessary. But the villagers over the years, no matter their true opinions of the steps, agreed that all the stone workers had one characteristic in common. They were the most determined people anyone had ever seen.

Work on the steps was much slower than the technological progress that now seemed to come in leaps and bounds. Flying machines, oddities at first, became commonplace. It wasn't long before a few daring and enterprising men and women from the village learned to fly. Before long it was easy for many people to see the village from the air, an even more dramatic vantage point than the mountaintop. But the stone workers didn't stop.

The people in the village were now the great-grandchildren of those who had been alive when the very first stonemason had carved the very first step. Now the steps went far up the side of the mountain. So far, in fact, that the top steps were often obscured whenever clouds covered the mountain.

Over the years, nearly fifty stone carvers had contributed their toil and sweat, and sometimes their blood, to the steps. Except when snow, wind, rain, or cold had made it impossible, the work continued. Now the steps were so far up the mountain that the last stone worker was forced to camp on the slope.

One day he walked into the village mayor's office, disheveled and worn, his face burned brown by the sun, and his hands callused from hard work. The man presented an old mallet and a worn steel chisel to the mayor.

"The work is done," the stonemason announced. "These tools belonged to the first stonemason. They have been handed down each time another mason took up the task. They are our gift to the village, now that the work is done."

So saying, the stonemason left the village and was never seen again.

The people of the village were astonished. No one had ever expected that the steps would be carved to the top of the highest peak. Some did not believe that it was actually completed, thinking that the last stonemason had simply abandoned the task.

There was, of course, only one way to learn the truth.

The mayor appointed two young men to climb the steps, and record their ascent with cameras. After much officious fanfare, the trek began. The process was not easy. A ladder had to be constructed and carried up each step, since each was half as tall as a man and just as wide and deep.

After two days the young men gained the summit and photographed the village. At that moment the first stonemason's dream was realized. Two days later they finished the descent. The steps, they reported, did in fact reach to the top of the highest peak.

The photographs of each of the hundreds of steps were put on display, and the villagers flocked to see them. Most popular was the one that showed the steps in one long, continuous undulating line up the mountainside, and disappearing into a cloud. It would, in time, come to be the trademark of the village. But there was one remarkable detail about each step that everyone was quick to notice. It explained why one stone worker after another had come to take up the task.

At the base of each step, there were two carved words: KEEP GOING.

CLOSING

The young man had one more question. "Will I ever understand life and death the way you do?"

"If you live long enough, yes," replied the old man. "There are times when I wish that I could understand some things more clearly. But my journey is not yet over. So perhaps I have something more to learn. I do know this: If you understand life, you understand death."

"What's to understand?" the young man retorted. "As far as I'm concerned, my father died before his time. Why couldn't death have waited?"

"Death is not to blame," pointed out the old man. "It was the disease that took your father. Death is often the consequence of choices we make. Someone decides to drive under the influence of alcohol and misses a curve he has driven hundreds of times. But, in truth, we begin dying the day we are born. That truth frightens most people because they have been taught that death is the enemy.

"My father—your great-grandfather—was a healer, in the old ways of our people. Before he died he told my mother he only wanted to be buried in a coffin made of wood. My father wanted his body to return to the Earth from which it came, without impediment. Many people look on death as the end. He looked on it as the end of one journey and the beginning of the next. He believed that a metal coffin is a denial of death, because it prevents remains from returning to the Earth. If you visit just about any cemetery in this country, you see that this society denies death. People bury their loved ones in marble, granite, or steel crypts, thinking it's a final act of love that they can give. Because of what my father taught me, I see it as preventing the end of the Earthly journey. And it affects the beginning of the spirit's journey to the next world.

"My father was not afraid of death, though I think he was sometimes afraid of life, as we all are at times. He was afraid of failure, of illness, of life without my mother. He was often afraid that perhaps he had not done his best in one situation or another. But he was never afraid to die.

"We may die by accident, disease, in war, from old age, at the hand of someone, or by our own hand. The manner of our death is often the last judgment others make of us. But I think if we are to be judged, it should be for how we lived.

"Your father was a good man; he lived a good life. You should not waste effort on anger over the way he died; celebrate the way he lived instead. That is his legacy, not the manner of his death."

The old man and his grandson sat quietly in the shade of the old cottonwood, listening to the gentle breeze rustling the leaves. The young man was awed by his grandfather's enormous strength of spirit, and grateful for the words that had given him peace in his time of anguish and confusion.

"I can't thank you enough, Grandpa," he said. "One day I hope I can be half as wise as you are. Thank you for all you have said."

"My grandfather spoke much the same words to me many times during the course of my journey. He reminded me often, as I remind you now; there is another Grandfather. Remember that in our language Grandfather also refers to the Great Power others call God. The words I spoke are really from that Grandfather, because of the journey that He gave me and helped me to make. The journey that has been my life is the source of what little wisdom I have gained.

"That Grandfather is all around. He is in the storm that challenges you, and in the strength that enables you to face it. He is that whisper of hope against despair, and the sunshine on your face when you meet each new day. He is there with you in your victories and embraces you when you suffer defeat. He was there when you came into this world to begin this journey, and He will be there when you leave it to begin your next one."

Once again the young man sat silently absorbing his grandfather's words. Then he whispered, "Thank you, Grandfather."

And he would always remember how the breeze grew stronger and rustled the cottonwood leaves louder, even if only for a moment. In the rustling of the leaves he thought he heard a soft, strong voice speaking in a lilting rhythm. As yet the words were not clear to him.

"Grandpa, do you hear the voice in the leaves?" he asked.

Old Hawk smiled. "Of course," he replied softly.

"What is it saying?"

"It is life speaking," replied the old man. "It says simply to Keep Going."

A young man asked his grandfather why life had to be so difficult sometimes. This was the old man's reply.

Grandfather says this: "In life there is sadness as well as joy, losing as well as winning, falling as well as standing, hunger as well as plenty, badness as well as goodness. I do not say this to make you despair, but to teach you reality. Life is a journey sometimes walked in light, sometimes in shadow."

Grandfather says this: "You did not ask to be born, but you are here. You have weaknesses as well as strengths. You have both because in life there is two of everything. Within you is the will to win, as well as the willingness to lose. Within you is the heart to feel compassion as well as the smallness to be arrogant. Within you is the way to face life as well as the fear to turn away from it."

Grandfather says this: "Life can give you strength. Strength can come from facing the storms of life, from knowing loss, feeling sadness and heartache, from falling into the depths of grief. You must stand up in the storm. You must face the wind and the cold and the darkness. When the storm blows hard you must stand firm, for it is not trying to knock you down, it is really trying to teach you to be strong."

Grandfather says this: "Being strong means taking one more step toward the top of the hill, no matter how weary you may be. It means letting the tears flow through the grief. It means to keep looking for the answer, though the darkness of despair is all around you. Being strong means to cling to hope for one more heartbeat, one more sunrise. Each step, no matter how difficult, is one more step closer to the top of the hill. To keep hope alive for one more heartbeat at a time leads to the light of the next sunrise, and the promise of a new day."

Grandfather says this: "The weakest step toward the top of the hill, toward sunrise, toward hope, is stronger than the fiercest storm."

Grandfather says this: "Keep going."

⌗

The Keep Going Prayer

Father Sky,
It is I who raises my voice to you,
Have pity on me.
Mother Earth,
It is I who raises my voice to you,
Have pity on me.
To all my relations who live to the West, North, East, and South,
It is I who raises my voice to you,
Have pity on me.
Grandfather,
It is I who raises my voice to you,
Have pity on me.
Thank you for the blessings and the difficulties I have known,
Because everything is the source of strength and wisdom.
You who knows the journey that waits for me,
Help me to face the path ahead,
Help me to find the strength to keep going,
No matter the difficulty, no matter how weary I may be.
Help me to face each day,
Help me to face each test, each storm,
One step at a time.
Grandfather,
I ask this in the name of
All my relations.

Acknowledgments

EVERYTHING HAS A BEGINNING, and that is no less true of this book. *Keep Going* began as a simple one-page text. That text was a consequence of my family enduring difficult times. During those days and months of difficulty, I recalled the advice given to me by all my grandparents—the Reverend Charles J. and Blanche Marshall, and Albert and Annie Two Hawk. All of them, as well as my parents, were deeply spiritual. Most frequently, I recalled my childhood with my maternal grandparents, and their influence on me—which is considerable. I recalled most often the conversations I had with my maternal grandfather. Bits and pieces of those conversations evolved into the one-page text.

This work is based on their insights, their experiences, their love, and their wisdom. So I thank them all, again, for everything they have done for me.

My mother, Hazel, has always been a source of quiet inspiration. She helped raised eight sons and three daughters, and found a way to keep going after my father died in 2001. She is still going strong, well into her eighth decade. *Ina, iyotancila.*

My wife, Connie, has been an inspiration in her own right. Not to mention that she is my literary agent and chief motivator. She was the first to believe in *Keep Going*, and worked tirelessly for several years to find the right publisher.

And that publisher was Sterling, in the person of Patricia Gift, Vice President and Editorial Director; and most importantly, our special friend.

The words in this book are mine, as are any short-comings. The heart and soul of it comes from all whom I've mentioned herein. There are no shortcomings there.

I thank you all.

Joseph M. Marshall III

About the Author

JOSEPH MARSHALL III is a Sicangu Lakota, born and raised on the Rosebud Sioux Reservation. In his career he has been a teacher and an educational and health programs administrator for the Rosebud Sioux tribe. He is one of the founders and a charter board member of Sinte Gleska University.

In addition to writing, he helps teach seminars on management and leadership, and has developed and teaches a course based on the leadership principles of Crazy Horse.

As a speaker, he has lectured to audiences across this country, as well as in France, Sweden, and Siberia.

His Web site is www.thunderdreamers.com.